KRAKOW

Travel with Marco Polo Insider Tips

INSIDER TIP
Your shortcut to a great experience

MARCO POLO TOP HIGHLIGHTS

COLLEGIUM MAIUS ★1

An academic jewel: one of the oldest universities in the world.

➤ p. 36, Sightseeing

KOŚCIOŁ FRANCISZKANÓW (FRANCISCAN CHURCH) ★2

Don't miss the city's only art nouveau church.

📷 *Tip: Visit the interior on a sunny day, when the works of art seem to compete with each other in their splendour.*

➤ p. 36, Sightseeing

KOŚCIÓŁ MARIACKI (ST MARY'S CHURCH) ★3

A testimony to the wealth of the Middle Ages – in particular the magnificent main altar by Veit Stoss.

➤ p. 33, Sightseeing

MUZEUM CZARTORYSKICH (CZARTORYSKI MUSEUM) ★4

Leonardo da Vinci's *Lady with an Ermine* sits amid the splendour of Kraków's oldest museum.

➤ p. 39, Sightseeing

RYNEK GŁÓWNY (MARKET SQUARE) ★5

The ever-young heart of the city: Europe's largest Gothic square.

📷 *Tip: Capture the sheer scale of the square from the tower of St Mary's Church.*

➤ p. 32, Sightseeing

SUKIENNICE (CLOTH HALL & ART MUSEUM) 6
Its Renaissance façade crowns Kraków's Market Square
Tip: The building's arches are the perfect backdrop for a shot of Rynek Główny. It's best at the blue hour – that moment when the sun dips below the horizon.

➤ p. 34, Sightseeing, p. 77, Shopping

ZAMEK KRÓLEWSKI (ROYAL CASTLE) 7
The country's most stunning Renaissance castle has more than its fair share of treasures within its walls (photo).
Tip: Head to the banks of the Vistula for a beautiful shot of the castle in all its glory, with river and ships in the foreground.

➤ p. 45, Sightseeing

KOŚCIÓŁ BOŻEGO CIAŁA (CORPUS CHRISTI CHURCH) 8
Red brick and gilded altars: this Kazimierz church is endlessly impressive. Make sure to spot the pulpit shaped like a boat.

➤ p. 50, Sightseeing

AUSCHWITZ-BIRKENAU 9
Moving, shocking, painful – and important: a visit to the former Nazi extermination camp.
Tip: Take the time to absorb your surroundings – not everything has to be photographed.

➤ p. 56, Sightseeing

FESTIWAL KULTURY ŻYDOWSKIEJ (FESTIVAL OF JEWISH CULTURE) 10
The Jewish world takes centre stage for a few days, with Poland's best artists and musicians.

➤ p. 93, Festivals & events

CONTENTS

⏲	Plan a trip
£–£££	Price categories
(*)	Premium-rate phone number
☂	Rainy day activities
🐖	Budget activities
👧	Family activities
⚑	Classic experiences

(🗺 A2) Refers to the removable pull-out map
(🗺 a2) Additional inset maps on the pull-out map
(0) Address located off the pull-out map

Krakus Mound

BEST OF KRAKÓW

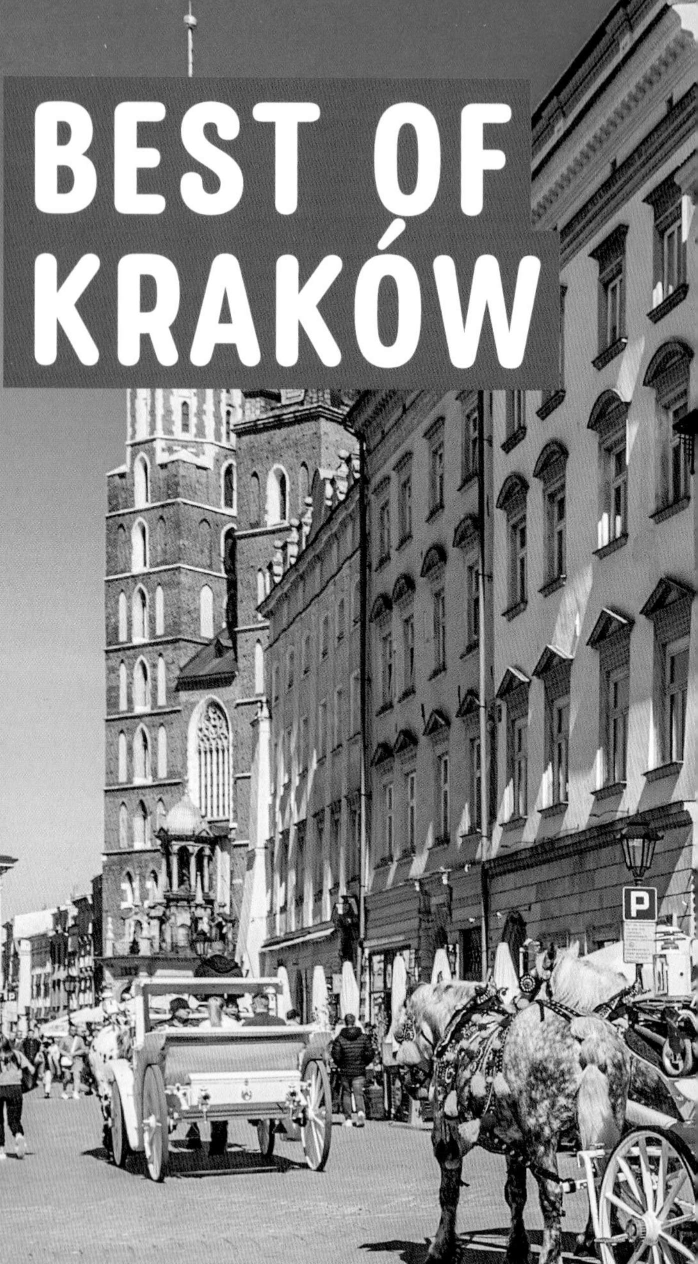

Travel in style around picturesque Rynek Główny

Wesele

BEST WHEN IT RAINS

ACTIVITIES TO BRIGHTEN YOUR DAY

VISIT AN ANIMAL-LOVING LADY

While a trip to see the *Mona Lisa* at the Louvre means braving the Paris crowds, in Kraków you can admire her lesser-known sister in a far more relaxed fashion: Leonardo da Vinci's *Lady with an Ermine* can be seen at the *Muzeum Czartoryskich*.

➤ p. 39, Sightseeing

DISCOVER A NEW HOBBY

On a sunny day, the sunlight streams through Kraków's panes in a kaleidoscope of colours – stained-glass windows are something of a symbol of the city. If it's raining, take refuge at the *Muzeum Witrażu* and learn how to make your very own stained-glass treasure on one of their courses.

➤ p. 52, Sightseeing

WORLD WAR II

In *Oskar Schindler's Enamel Factory*, you can learn about the indescribable suffering of Kraków's Jewish and non-Jewish population during the Nazi occupation. You should allow yourself plenty of time for this moving experience (photo).

➤ p. 53, Sightseeing

FOLLOW THE YELLOW BRICK ROAD

Original brickwork from industrial buildings on the site has been integrated into the modern *Galeria Kazimierz* shopping centre. The brickwork's special charm – along with the cinemas, restaurants, cafés and children's play area – make this one of the city's most pleasant places to shop.

➤ p. 74, Shopping

DEEP CHILL

When it's really chucking it down, why not lounge at *Le Scandale* while you wait for the sun to return? Bring a good book and start the day with breakfast.

➤ p. 86, Nightlife

BEST ON A BUDGET

FOR SMALLER WALLETS

PANORAMIC CITY VIEW

Although lookout points over Kraków usually charge an entrance fee, in Podgórze, on top of the *Krakus Mound*, you'll discover a free panoramic view overlooking the beautiful Vistula river (photo).

➤ p. 22, Get to know Kraków

A TREAT FOR YOUR EARS

Enjoy a free concert in an environment made for classical music. Many *Kraków churches* put on incredible live music events, and don't charge a penny to attend.

➤ p. 29, Sightseeing

MONUMENTS IN THE PARK

It is hard to imagine a more beautiful site for a sculpture exhibition. Stroll through the *Planty*, the strip of parkland surrounding the Old Town, and admire one of the largest collections of 19th- and 20th-century monuments.

➤ p. 38, Sightseeing

MODERN ART ON A THURSDAY

To experience fascinating modern art for free, head to *MOCAK* early on a Thursday. The free tickets are a hot commodity and tend to go fairly quickly.

➤ p. 53, Sightseeing

PARTY ON A BUDGET

For those with slim wallets but sufficient energy to want to dance the night away, most Kraków clubs don't charge an admission fee after 1am.

➤ p. 82, Nightlife

FREE MUSEUMS

Whether it is the *Józef Mehoffer House*, the *National Museum (Muzeum Narodowe)* or the *Archaeological Museum* on the Wawel, once a week – usually Tuesday – you can visit many permanent collections without having to pay. Days do sometimes change, though, so check online for information before you head out!

➤ p. 118, Good to know

BEST WITH CHILDREN

FUN FOR YOUNG & OLD

MEET THE DOPPELGÄNGERS

Get up close with Shrek, Jack Sparrow, Wills and Kate or even Donald Trump! They won't have a lot to say – after all, this is the *Polonia Wax Museum*.

➤ p. 40. Sightseeing

A JOURNEY THROUGH TIME

Explore the wonders of evolution at the *Natural History Museum (Muzeum Przyrodnicze PAN)*, and come face to face with a global sensation: the fantastically preserved prehistoric woolly rhinoceros.

➤ p. 42, Sightseeing

ANIMALS IN THE FOREST

Set in the vast Wolski Forest, the location alone makes a trip to the petting zoo in the *Zoological Gardens (Ogród Zoologiczny)* here a thrilling adventure (photo).

➤ p. 56, Sightseeing

SWEET TREATS STILL WARM

Ever wondered how sweets are actually made? Or what they taste like when the caramel is still warm? Find the answers at live demonstrations at the *Ciuciu Cukier Artist* confectioners.

➤ p. 75, Shopping

FUN IN THE PARK

Kids still got energy to burn off after that city tour? Head to *Park Jordana*. As well as plenty of space to let off steam, children can have fun in pedalos, play football, enjoy the slides and climbing frames and so much more …

➤ p. 90, Sport & wellness

SOAKED TO THE BONE, BUT SMILES ALL ROUND

While the kids whizz down the water slides at *Aquapark*, parents can enjoy yoga or a sauna.

➤ p. 90, Sport & wellness

BEST

CLASSIC EXPERIENCES

ONLY IN KRAKÓW

IN THE HEART OF TOWN

The *Rynek Główny* is not only the largest Gothic square in Europe, but also one of the most beautiful. Climb the *Town Hall Tower* and be charmed by the architecture of Market Square below.

➤ p. 32, p. 36, Sightseeing

SUNKEN MEDIEVAL KRAKÓW

Delve deep into the history of the city at the *Rynek Podziemny (Rynek Underground).* Located beneath the Cloth Hall, this museum offers a mysteriously illuminated, detailed reconstruction of medieval Kraków.

➤ p. 35, Sightseeing

IN THE ASTRONOMER'S STUDY

Poland's oldest university had already been open for 130 years when Nicolaus Copernicus began his studies at the *Collegium Maius* in the 1490s. Touring its magnificent halls and chambers will take you back in time.

➤ p. 36, Sightseeing

GEFILTE FISH & KLEZMER

Experience Jewish history and culture like never before. At *Klezmer Hois*, you can enjoy an evening of Jewish food and the sounds of klezmer music, a genre combining many musical styles.

➤ p. 68, Eating & drinking

LIVE INTERNATIONAL JAZZ

Kraków is known for jazz, and international stars perform in the fabulous cellar setting of *Harris Piano Jazz Bar*. Recharge your batteries with some drinks and great music (photo)!

➤ p. 85, Nightlife

THE DANCING DRAGON

The legend lives on: Kraków's mythical Wavel Dragon – the subject of many local tales – can be seen everywhere in the city. It's also at the heart of the annual *Dragon Parade* in June, a celebration with concerts and family picnics along the Vistula river.

➤ p. 92, Festivals & events

GET TO KNOW KRAKÓW

Omnipresent, even on the city's walls: Pope John Paul II

DISCOVER KRAKÓW

Live like a local: soaking in the sun on Plac Nowy

Kraków's centuries-old, rich and eventful history is evident all around you, but visitors will find no trace of the stuffy museum-like atmosphere you might find in other similarly historic cities. The metropolis on the Vistula river is full of energy and exudes an almost Mediterranean-style *joie de vivre*.

THE MAGIC OF A FAIRYTALE CITY

The city appears to be charmed in more than one respect. It avoided destruction by invading armies and enemy forces for centuries and also became one of the most important centres of scholarship in Europe in the 14th and 15th centuries. These factors helped create a cultural and architectural gem. Kraków's unique atmosphere – a mixture of culture and vitality, of history and modernity, of future

957
Settlement first documented

1257
City rebuilt after destruction by Mongol invaders

1364
The university is founded

1385–1596
Golden age as capital under the Jagiellonian dynasty

1489
Sculptor Veit Stoss completes his altar at St Mary's

1734
The last royal coronation

1815-1846
Kraków is a free city, with political and economic independence

vision and past legends – draws a growing number of visitors each year to walk in Copernicus's footsteps, take part in festivals and make a journey through time amid historic architecture. Or perhaps simply to enjoy life in the restaurants, cafés and clubs that are on a par with those in much bigger cities.

UNSCATHED BEAUTY

Kraków has a big heart; in fact it is one of the world's largest: the Rynek Główny, the main square in the centre of the Old Town, measures $200m^2$. It's an open space that makes a huge impression, with the city's buildings arranged with the regularity of a chessboard around it. Kraków's heart is surrounded by absolute beauty, with houses and buildings of every conceivable architectural style and period, thanks to the fact that the metropolis on the Vistula has managed to survive the last 800 years more or less unscathed. City life revolves around this square; this is where Kraków locals meet and where the action is – action that takes place until late into the night and even deep under the ground.

IN THE VAULTS BENEATH YOUR FEET

Many of the more than 100 cafés, restaurants, bars and clubs around Rynek Główny that get Kraków's nightlife going with a swing – especially on warm summer evenings – are located in traditional brick vaults below street level. As in many old metropolises, street levels have changed over the centuries, due to earth deposits and layers of construction work, with ground floors sinking to

1850 The city goes up in flames

1941 A Jewish ghetto is created in Podgórze

1947 Construction starts on the steelworks in Nowa Huta

1978 The Old Town and Wawel are made UNESCO World Heritage Sites

2022 The city welcomes more than 120,000 refugees as war breaks out in Ukraine

2023 The right-wing conservative PiS party is voted out of office cellar level. You can get an insight into what this subterranean world looks like over a beer in one of the historic beer cellars. Take your cue from the local residents. They love going out, and the bars are full, whatever the time of day – a reflection of the common saying, "People work in Warsaw but live in Kraków."

A HAVEN FOR POETS, MUSICIANS AND PAINTERS

Kraków had a hard time getting over the fact that the royal court moved to its unloved sister, which then became the capital, 400 years ago. However, the city compensated for its fall into relative unimportance in its own way: it became a magical city, the protector of stories and legends, the patron of poets, musicians and painters. The fact that Kraków is considered to be Poland's cultural capital is not only due to the splendour of its architectural monuments, which led to the entire centre being named a UNESCO World Heritage Site. Its reputation is further supported by the large number of theatres, concert halls, galleries and museums to be found in what – with a population of around 800,000 – is a relatively small city. In addition, there is a jazz scene that connoisseurs consider comparable only with New York's. We should also not forget klezmer music, the traditional Jewish folk music, which is as vibrant as ever and underlines Kraków's importance as a former centre of Jewish life in Europe.

JEWISH HERITAGE AND CONTEMPORARY LIFE

Kraków's Jewish heritage is concentrated in Kazimierz; the formerly independent town was incorporated in 1800. The mainly peaceful coexistence with the Catholic neighbours lasted until the German occupation of Poland in 1939. Only around 5,000 of the 60,000 Jews living in Kazimierz survived the Nazi horror. Before the German invasion, Kraków's Jews had formed 25% of the population. Director Steven Spielberg paid tribute to their suffering, as well as to industrialist Oskar Schindler, who saved more than 1,100 forced labourers from being murdered, in his film *Schindler's List*. Today, Kazimierz has managed to preserve its unique flair and, like everywhere else in Poland, the Jewish community is growing here too. It is a youthful, hip district, popular with students, artists and party-goers, who have fun all night in summer and hunt for retro chic at the flea markets during the daytime.

A HISTORIC UNIVERSITY CITY

Despite being many centuries old, Kraków emanates a feeling of youthful freshness. Its approximately 130,000 students make it a young city. Newer state and private universities have taken their place alongside the oldest university in Poland and one of the oldest in the world – Jagiellonian University, founded in 1364. Wawel Hill, with the tourist highlights of Wawel Royal Castle and Wawel Cathedral, was originally settled more than 50,000 years ago. There is proof that salt mining was carried out near Kraków from around 1400 BCE.

AT A GLANCE

802,000
Population

Leeds: 822,500

200
Churches and chapels

London's financial centre, the City of London: 50

16km^2
of parks and green spaces

Leeds area: 40km^2

HIGHEST POINT: PIŁSUDSKI HILL
383m

An artificial hill in the Wolski Forest

WARMEST MONTH
JULY
19.5°C

THE NUMBER OF PIGEONS ON CITY STREETS AND SQUARES
40,000

A LOCAL SNACK

150,000 traditional Kraków pretzels, *obwarzanek*, are sold daily at around 200 stalls

CHAKRA

A magical stone emanating spiritual energy is said to be hidden on Wawel Hill

SIGISMUND BELL
12 bell ringers are needed to ring the bell

SCIENCE FICTION GURU
STANISŁAW LEM LIVED IN KRAKÓW UNTIL HIS LAST DAYS

TRADING TIMES

Kraków was first mentioned in a document in 965, indicating that the settlement on Wawel Hill had developed into an important trading centre at the intersection of a number of major trade routes. The settlement grew, became an episcopal see and capital city, and also survived devastating strikes by the Mongols in the 13th century. Kraków experienced its heyday in the 15th and 16th centuries, which is clearly visible in the magnificent Renaissance architecture. The city attracted artists, progressive thinkers and scholars. Nicolaus Copernicus, who would later create a new view of the universe, was just one of the many who studied at Jagiellonian University, staying there until 1494.

CHURCHES BURSTING WITH TREASURES

There are more than 400 sights within the Planty, the green belt encircling the Old Town. They include townhouses, palaces, famous museums with collections of international and Polish art and, last but not least, 17 churches. The number of houses of worship funded by monarchs, the nobility and other rich citizens provides striking evidence of the city's wealth. The world-famous treasures found in the churches, such as the altarpiece created by sculptor Veit Stoss for St Mary's Church, attract art lovers and pilgrims alike.

A STEELWORKS AS A BULWARK AGAINST THE BOURGEOISIE

Kraków has always been a centre of religious life in Poland. In the past, the city played a significant role as a diocese and site of the coronation of the country's kings. Kraków is often called a "papal city", although Karol Wojtyła, who became Pope John Paul II, was not born here (he was from Wadowice). Nonetheless, Wojtyła spent more than 40 years in Kraków and left an indelible mark on the city, opposing the anti-religious communist regime in post-war Poland. Kraków and communism is an interesting consideration in itself, and it is hard to imagine two more opposing mindsets. On the one hand, you have a city of liberals, freethinkers and dissenters; on the other, you have a regime that saw no place for these bourgeois tendencies in its classless society. To take the wind out of the sails of the liberal-minded bourgeois resistance, those in power built the district of Nowa

Collegium Maius: where Nicolaus Copernicus studied astronomy

Huta and a steel mill to go along with it. In doing so, they hoped to create a settlement for proletarian workers. Their plans backfired, however, and the complete opposite happened. It was precisely these workers and their strong adherence to the Catholic Church that finally brought about the collapse of the system.

STUDENTS AND TOURISTS ARE REMAKING THE CITY

Today, the steel plant is a thing of the past. The people living here have come to terms with the upheaval caused by the end of communism and the opening up of the country in the 1990s. Today, Kraków lives from tourism, its service sector and its university. The city is the largest employer in the region and, for years now, Kraków has been able to boast unemployment rates far below the national average – it's currently less than 2.5%. Since the end of the Covid pandemic, millions of visitors once again come to pay their respects to Leonardo da Vinci's *Lady with an Ermine*, admire the Cloth Hall in Market Square, stroll through Nowa Huta and see Kazimierz. Kraków's inhabitants are fully aware that they live in a very special city – and they are proud of the fact. They love and cultivate its history and traditions and know how to celebrate these for days on end – no matter whether the festivities are religious or of a more worldly nature. It is also said that the locals are thrifty, if not downright stingy. That may well be true, but they are also hospitable and cosmopolitan, qualities the locals have shown since the very start of the war in Ukraine. Today, around a quarter of the city's inhabitants are Ukrainian refugees.

UNDERSTAND KRAKÓW

MOUNDS OF MYSTERY

Is it really true that the *Wanda Mound (Kopiec Wandy)* in Nowa Huta and the *Krakus Mound (Kopiec Krakusa)* in Podgórze are part of an astronomical calendar? Well, it is true that on certain Celtic and Slavic holidays, if you're standing on one of the two mounds, the sun sets and rises directly above the other one. Some claim the Krakus Mound (16m high) is the tomb of Kraków's legendary founder, Krakus, while the other one belongs to his daughter. Even archaeologists say the mounds' elevations date back to pre-Christian times and were artificially raised. There are two more man-made mounds located around Kraków: *Piłsudski's Mound*, created in 1937, and *Kościuszko's Mound*, from 1820. Both are named after Polish national heroes. The latter is especially worth visiting; from the mound's summit, you'll have a particularly beautiful view of the city.

LEGENDS GALORE!

It's rarely a good idea to dine on lamb stuffed with sulphur, tar and pepper. As unusual as this meal may sound, it plays an important role in Kraków's most famous fairytale. The story's bad guy is a cave-dwelling dragon at the foot of *Wawel Hill*. In the story, he feeds on the city's virgins, which are sacrificed to him. This changes, however, when a brave cobbler appears and serves him this dish of lamb with its unusual stuffing. As he eats, the fire-breathing dragon gets an unbearably upset stomach. He drinks from the Vistula to soothe the pain, but he ends up drinking himself to the point of combustion. In the end, this unappetising meal won the cobbler the princess's hand in marriage. But, despite his bravery, the city gave the dragon the true fame and glory – on Rynek Główny (Market Square) you can buy stuffed versions of him at every stand, and in summer colourful depictions of him parade through the city.

Kraków is a city full of myths, fairytales and legends. The pigeons on Rynek Główny, for example, are said to have once been knights, so no one ever dares to drive them away. According to the myth, a witch turned them into birds after their master failed to pay her back the money she had lent him. Then there's the trumpet call, the *hejnał*. It can be heard on the hour from St Mary's Church, in commemoration of the 13th-century Mongol invasion of Poland. The attention to historical detail is impressive: the call stops right at the moment the Polish trumpeter was hit by an arrow as he played his warning. Next, we have the *Lajkonik*, a man dressed in Mongol attire, who also symbolises the invasion. In summer, he walks across the square trying to touch everyone with his sceptre. Let him – it's said to bring good luck!

Kraków has jazz in its blood; not a day goes by without a live gig somewhere in the city

ALL KINDS OF JAZZ

Without jazz, the city on the Vistula would be without its heart. Kraków, is the capital of Polish jazz, and you seem to hear it everywhere – in cafés, restaurants and clubs. The first real jazz bands began playing here almost 100 years ago and little has changed ever since.

Imported from the US, jazz was forbidden in communist Poland, but never truly disappeared. It was played in secret up until 1954, but in the 1960s jazz festivals rekindled the flame, and it's now inextinguishable.

INSIDER TIP
Give jazz a chance!

Even if you're not a jazz fan, you should give it a chance in Kraków. You'll hear a mellow, almost classical version of it at *Piano Rouge*. At *U Muniaka* and *Alchemia*, they play more experimental and modern jazz that's free spirited, avant-garde and somewhat punk-like. At *Club Prozak 2.0*, the jazz is easy to dance to. Finally, you'll hear spontaneous jam sessions in pubs like *Piec Art*.

DANCE THE KLEZMER

If it's not jazz being played in Kraków, it must be klezmer – the city's "second sound", if you like. It may not be as hip as the jazz originating from the US, but it's a lot older. The first texts mentioning the *klezmorim* (travelling musicians who played traditional Jewish music) date from the 15th century. Later, klezmer was influenced by the music played at Ashkenazi Jewish weddings in eastern Europe and by the joyous Sinti and Roma music from Ukraine, Russia and

Bulgaria. Klezmer was brought to the US by eastern European Jewish immigrants, where it developed further. It was especially popular at the beginning of the 20th century, and from there, the genre took on a new form. Today, the music's evolution has long since matured, but some musicians still create new styles by combining it with jazz.

In both Kraków and the rest of Poland, many young bands like *Kroke (kroke.pl/en)* and the *Bester Quartet* are following in their ancestors' footsteps and even play the traditional klezmer instruments (clarinet, violin and drums). You'll hear them in synagogues, restaurants, at the *Galicia Jewish Museum* (see p. 49), *Klezmer-Hois* (see p. 68), the *Klezmer Music Venue (Sławkowska 14 | cracowconcerts.com/klezmer-music)* and during the *Jewish Culture Festival* (see p. 93).

View from the Vistula to the Wawel

THIS RIVER HAS IT ALL!

The Vistula river, known as the Wisła in Polish, is one of Kraków's biggest tourist attractions. Although it's forbidden to swim in it, it's still a popular place for water sports and boat excursions (see p. 118), for example to the Benedictine Abbey in Tyniec. During the summer months, the Vistula becomes a great place for partying. The locals really enjoy being near the river, so much so that they dock their boats and spend the entire day just eating, drinking and dancing. If you're intending to visit overnight, you can stay in one of the hotels floating on the water. You'll find that most of the boat moorings are at the bottom of Wawel Hill and in Kazimierz on Bulwar Czerwieński.

On the other bank, Bulwar Wołyński, you'll find a sandy beach and a floating swimming pool. Many festivals are held along the Vistula, and it's a popular place for families to picnic. If you want to go for a walk or a jog, the loveliest area is the section between Wawel Hill and the bridge in Podgórze *(Most Piłsudskiego)*. A pedestrian bridge *(Kładka Bernatka)*, which is illuminated at night, connects Kazimierz with Podgórze.

AT THE COFFEE HOUSE

Sitting in a coffee house is not only an

essential part of any visit to Kraków but also a way to travel back in time and immerse yourself in the wonderfully nostalgic coffee-house atmosphere. Coffee houses take you back to the 19th century, a time when Kraków was part of the Kingdom of Galicia and Lodomeria (named for the east European, rather than Spanish, Galicia region). The kingdom included the Grand Duchy of Kraków, the Duchy of Zator and the Duchy of Auschwitz, and was part of the Habsburg Empire between 1772 and 1918. Today, the region belongs to Ukraine and Poland.

Austrian influence is visible in cafés like *Kawiarnia Noworolski* (see p. 63) or *Kawiarnia Europejska (Krzysztofory Palace Rynek Główny 35)*, which feel just as authentic as *Hawełka* (see p. 66), a restaurant with the title of "Purveyor to the Imperial and Royal Court". The horse-drawn carriages on Market Square are also reminiscent of Vienna, the city that inspired Kraków's art and architecture in the 19th century. The impact was so great that the restaurant *Pod Złotą Pipą (Ulica Floriańska 30)* even placed the Austrian Emperor Franz Josef on its sign. Today, he watches over the guests as they enjoy their meals in the restaurant's Gothic cellar.

This was an economically hard time for Kraków. Culturally speaking, however, the province enjoyed a large degree of freedom. Art, cabaret, Polish theatre and literature all flourished.

THE POPE'S CREAM CAKE

When you take a coffee break while exploring the city, order a piece of

TRUE OR FALSE?

YOU HAVE TO COME OVER!

The ever-hospitable Poles? As hackneyed as the reports may be, they really are true: strike up a conversation with a Pole and, while they may seem cool at first, an invitation is an inevitability before too long. And once you head to their home, no cupboard or drawer will be left unemptied to meet your every need. And if you're young, the sheer number of students can mean lots of new friends!

NA ZDROWIE!

Statistically, Poles drink no more than many other nationalities. But perhaps they do it with greater panache! And with vodka, of course, which was actually invented in Poland. And these days the stereotype of bad Polish beer is a thing of the past: a buzzing craft beer scene is now firmly established in Kraków.

THE CAR'S GONE!

This rather unkind stereotype is also not true: Poland sees no more car thefts than any other big city. Still, there are plenty of reasons to avoid bringing your car to Kraków – not least the shortage of parking spaces along the winding medieval streets and alleyways. So if you do come back to find your car gone, it has probably been towed!

kremówka papieska. This delicious cream cake is named after Pope John Paul II (born in Wadowice) and nicknamed the "papal *kremówka*". According to legend, Karol Wojtyła (John Paul II's birth name) is said to have eaten 18 slices of these calorie bombs during a friendly bet.

From the Ulica Franciszkańska, you can see the "papal window" of the Bishop's Palace. It's always decorated with burning candles and white-yellow flowers in memory of Wojtyła. He was ordained as a priest in 1946 and became an archbishop in 1963. Together with the independent labour union Solidarity, Wojtyła stood against the communist rulers of Poland. John Paul II died in 2005 and was canonised in 2014; you'll find memorials of him throughout the city, and his legacy still lives on today.

A WORLD OF READING

If you're walking through Planty park and see someone on a bench with a phone to their ear, they may not be talking. They may very well be listening to novels from Nobel Prize winners. Since 2013, when Kraków became one of UNESCO's cities of literature, QR codes have been inset onto benches with links to audio books, not just in Planty but in Kazimierz and Nowa Huta too. Anyone who scans the code on the benches' backrest will receive information on the life and work of Polish Nobel Laureates of Literature, as well as audio book links to their works. Writers featured include Wisława Szymborska, Czesław Miłosz (both of whom lived in Kraków), and many others. Visit *kody.miasto literatury.pl* to find an interactive map indicating at least 180 literary park benches, as well as cafés, bookshops and other places related to literature.

INSIDER TIP
Literary park benches

Those who love books will also be impressed with Kraków in general. The first bookshop in Europe opened here in 1610! Today, the city offers plenty of bookstores and second-hand bookshops. In addition to two literature festivals, Kraków also hosts the country's largest international book fair. Visit *krakowcityofliterature.com* for more information.

BOOMTOWN

If you've ever wondered whether the increasing number of vegan and vegetarian restaurants in a city has anything to do with its air quality, Kraków has the answer – yes, it does. Here's how. For years, the city has been attracting tech and service companies from all over the world, and it's created a booming economy. Members of the young and well-educated "Google generation" are moving to the city on the Vistula from all over Europe. More and more foreign students are also coming here: a total of around 130,000 young people attend the 23 universities in Kraków. The districts of Zabłocie, where many students live, and Podgórze are all the rage.

A boom in vegan and vegetarian restaurants, along with galleries, bars and clubs cater for this demographic. But while the economic boom may have put Kraków on a par with cities like Paris or Berlin in some respects, it is making it more expensive and has also created increased traffic, which is having an effect on the city's air quality – hence the link with vegetarian restaurants. Luckily, the city has recognised the problem and is taking measures against the smog.

KRAKÓW'S ARTISTIC DUO

Two great artists left their mark on Kraków at completely different times – one in the 15th and the other in the 19th century. Veit Stoss came to Kraków from Nuremberg in 1477. It is not really known where the sculptor and painter learned his art, nor which works he created before leaving Nuremberg. It was his monumental altar for St Mary's Church in Kraków that made him famous. The 13m-high and 11m-wide altar is considered one of the great masterpieces of Gothic carving. After 19 years in Kraków, he left the city as a highly respected citizen and returned to Nuremberg, where he created many other masterpieces before his death in 1533.

The main artistic personality of the fin-de-siècle at the close of the 19th century was Stanisław Wyspiański, a man who could turn his hand to many things. He studied in Paris and made a name for himself as a painter and writer. He also designed furniture and complete interiors, the sets for his plays, and stained-glass windows, including those in the Franciscan Church. Nature, simple peasant life and Polish history are the leitmotifs of his creative work.

Memorial to Pope John Paul II, who spent over 40 years in Kraków

SIGHT SEEING

Kraków's historic centre is small, charming and easy to explore on foot. Here, you can take a walk or a carriage ride back to the days of the Austrian Habsburg Empire.

The centre initially seems to be dominated by the city's past. The Wawel complex towers over the Old Town and includes the Royal Castle and a magnificent cathedral. Church towers dot Kraków's skyline, and impressive sights are visible both on and off the Royal Route. The scenery changes, however, as you walk through Planty, the park that encircles the Old Town. Here, in the place where the

You'll find all the venues in this chapter on the pull-out map

Modern life with a historic backdrop on Kraków's Market Square

city's medieval walls once stood, you'll discover plenty of paths as well as magnificent areas to relax in. The Vistula also offers many leisure activities. You can take a river cruise, rent a paddle boat or enjoy a meal at one of the riverboat restaurants. And on Rynek Główny, the city's main square, life remains lively and vibrant, with something of a Mediterranean vibe.

You can head to many of the city's churches for free classical music concerts – just look out for posters with information and event dates (*wstęp wolny* means "admission free").

THE DISTRICTS AT A GLANCE

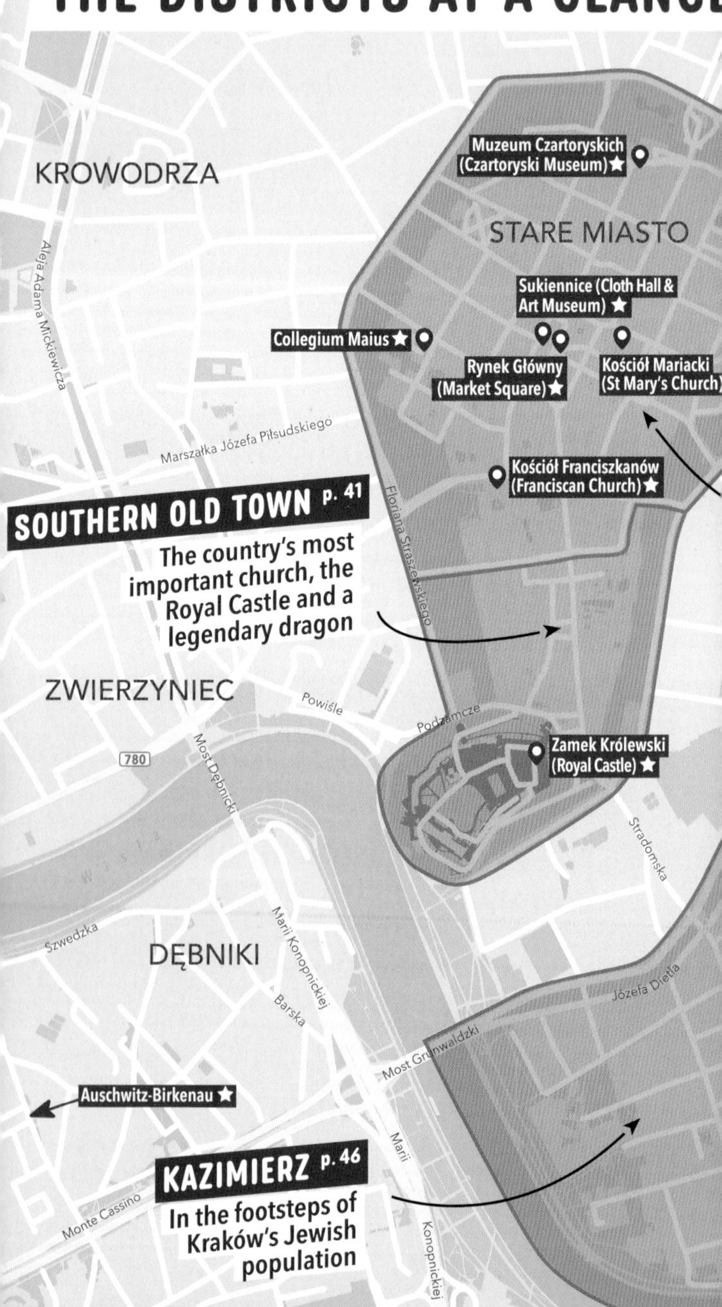

MARCO POLO HIGHLIGHTS

★ RYNEK GŁÓWNY (MARKET SQUARE)
Feel the city's magic on this expansive, historic square. ➤ p. 32

★ KOŚCIÓŁ MARIACKI (ST MARY'S CHURCH)
Wealth, splendour and the famous altar by Veit Stoss. ➤ p. 33

★ SUKIENNICE (CLOTH HALL & ART MUSEUM)
The magnificent hall on Market Square. ➤ p. 34, p. 77

★ KOŚCIÓŁ FRANCISZKANÓW (FRANCISCAN CHURCH)
An art nouveau gem. ➤ p. 36

★ COLLEGIUM MAIUS
Kraków's oldest university building. ➤ p. 36

★ MUZEUM CZARTORYSKICH (CZARTORYSKI MUSEUM)
Even better after renovations. The country's oldest museum has one of Europe's most valuable art collections. ➤ p. 39

★ ZAMEK KRÓLEWSKI (ROYAL CASTLE)
A Renaissance gem packed with treasures. ➤ p. 45

★ KOŚCIÓŁ BOŻEGO CIAŁA (CORPUS CHRISTI CHURCH)
Monumental Gothic splendour. ➤ p. 50

★ FABRYKA SCHINDLERA (SCHINDLER FACTORY)
Thought-provoking exhibition on the Nazi occupation. ➤ p. 53

★ AUSCHWITZ-BIRKENAU
Never forget. An essential confrontation with the horror wreaked by the Nazis. ➤ p. 56

Kraków's many districts outside the Old Town, such as Kazimierz, Zwierzyniec and Kleparz, fan out from Planty park.

They are usually easy to walk to from the Old Town, and so we have only listed trams and buses in cases where walking would be a stretch.

NORTHERN OLD TOWN

There's always a lot going on in this part of Kraków. You'll stroll past high-end restaurants and the most exclusive shops and boutiques.

Be happy you're visiting Kraków today and not a few centuries ago. At that time, restrictions meant it was impossible to stroll through Kraków's beautiful Gothic city centre. Even if you were well known or of high rank, visitors were never allowed to veer from Królewska, the Royal Route. Still, that was not all that bad, as the Route passed the city's most significant and exciting buildings. Today, the Route starts at St Florian's Gate, goes down Ulica Floriańska and leads into the city centre. It crosses Rynek Główny and goes uphill to the Wawel complex, which includes the castle and Cathedral. Still undamaged by all the wars the city went through, Kraków's most beautiful churches, palaces and buildings stand today to tell of the city's history. They were mostly built between the 13th and 15th centuries during the city's golden age, when Kraków was the country's largest city.

> **WHERE TO START?**
>
> The main square, **Rynek Główny** *(▥ c3–4)*, is the best place to start your sightseeing tour as it is at the heart of the city. The square is pedestrianised for the most part, but you can park your car either on a side street *(parking tickets at machines: 6 zł per hour, free Sun and after 8pm)*, at the car park near the Franciscan Church *(Plac Wszystkich Świętych 5)* or at Westerplatte 18. All tram lines will take you into the centre of town.

1 RYNEK GŁÓWNY (MARKET SQUARE) ★ ⚑

"Windows? No thank you!" It's hard to believe, but this is how the wealthiest citizens thought back when they had their residences and palaces built around Market Square. You may also be surprised by the buildings' narrow facades. They were constructed this way so the rich could avoid paying higher taxes. Back then, taxes were calculated depending on how many windows a building had. This is why you'll sometimes see buildings with no more than two windows – just enough to let the light in! A rather unusual look for the largest medieval square in Europe, at 200m^2.

Kraków's fascinating Market Square never sleeps, and has always been the city's cultural hub. In the summer, it's a place that almost feels like Italy – not only because of the pigeons, but also for the Renaissance architecture of the

Sukiennice (Cloth Hall) and the residential buildings. The Cloth Hall and *St Mary's Church* are among the Market Square's highlights. Until the 19th century, the square was strewn with grocery stores, large and small buildings, and the town hall. However, these were demolished in 1820. Today, the townhouses on the square show an array of architectural styles – from Gothic to 20th century. All year round, the square puts on festivals, concerts and exhibitions. Seasonal markets are held at Christmas and Easter. *c3–4*

2 KOŚCIÓŁ ŚW. WOJCIECHA (ST ADALBERT'S CHURCH)

Possibly Kraków's smallest and oldest church dates from the 11th century. Its greatest treasure is its crypt, which hosts an exhibition on Market Square's history. Exhibits show how the level of the plaza rose more than 2.5m over the centuries. Beautiful chamber concerts take place here regularly; the church has a capacity for an audience of 80 *(tickets on site). Museum: May–Oct Mon–Sat 10am–4pm | admission 7 zł | Rynek Główny 2 | c4*

3 KOŚCIÓŁ MARIACKI (ST MARY'S CHURCH) ★

St Mary's Church's stunning 14th-century *Kraków Altarpiece* was created by Veit Stoss. The artist came from Nuremberg, Germany, and devoted 12 years of his life to this masterpiece, beginning in 1477. Made of oak and lime, it measures 11m by 13m, and is decorated with gold leaf. The altar was recently renovated over a period of six years and has been restored to its original medieval design, including the colours chosen 500 years ago. In the south aisle, you'll find a statue of the crucified Christ. Stoss sculpted it from a single piece of sandstone.

St Mary's Church has been modified and expanded several times, which explains the variety of

Gothic splendour in St Mary's Church

architectural styles seen both in and outside the building.

You'll have the most beautiful view of the city from the church's 82m-high *tower (April–Oct Tue–Sat 10am–5.30am, Sun from 1pm, closed in bad weather | admission 20 zł)*. But tickets are limited, so it's best to get yours the day before or as soon as the church's ticket window opens (see below). It's also worth remembering there is no lift – you will have to make your own way up the 71 steps! Every hour on the hour, you'll hear the *hejnał*, known as Poland's second national anthem, being played from the higher of the two towers by a trumpet. *Mon–Sat 11.30am–6pm, Sun 2–6pm | admission to church 15 zł | Plac Mariacki 5 | mariacki.com | 🕮 d4*

INSIDER TIP
Book ahead for the tower

4 SUKIENNICE (CLOTH HALL & ART MUSEUM) ★

Cloth Hall, located in the middle of Market Square, is one of Kraków's many famous landmarks. It was the place where the city's most sought-after goods were traded, including salt and all kinds of fabric. Kraków used to be on an old salt-trading route and enjoyed special privileges, contributing to it becoming the wealthiest city in the Polish kingdom. The structure was initially erected in the 14th century and altered in the 16th and 19th centuries. The long hall has external arcades and an original Renaissance parapet adorned with grotesque gargoyles. The Cloth Hall still flourishes as a centre of commerce: in the souvenir shops on the ground floor, you can buy amber jewellery and other arts and crafts.

View of the Cloth Hall at the heart of Market Square

On the first floor, you'll find a gallery with 19th-century Polish painting and sculpture, *Galeria Sztuki Polskiej XIX wieku (Tue–Sun 10am–6pm | admission 32 zł,* 🐷 *free Tue, audio guide 7 zł, combined ticket for permanent exhibitions at all branches of the National Museum 120 zł, excluding the Czartoryski museum, see p. 52) | Rynek Główny 1–3 | mnk.pl |* ⏲ *1 hr).* It includes a wide collection of large historical paintings, Polish portraits and landscapes. The museum's *Café Szał (daily 10am–11pm)*, with a view of St Mary's Church from its terrace, is a joy for the senses.

INSIDER TIP
Café terrace views

Take a walk through medieval Kraków beneath Market Square at the ⚑ *Rynek Podziemny (Underground Market Square Museum, Mon, Wed/Thur 10am–7pm, Fri–Sun 10am–8pm | admission 32 zł, audio guide 5 zł,* 🐷 *Tue free admission (book early!) | Rynek Główny 1 | podziemiarynku.com |* ⏲ *1–2 hrs).* The cemetery and miniature versions of small shops that used to be here are especially fascinating. You will also be able to see objects unearthed during excavations under the square. Video on TV screens teaches you about the most important events in Kraków's history (available in English). *🕮 c4*

5 WIEŻA RATUSZOWA (TOWN HALL TOWER)

Although the climb to the top of this 14th-century, 70m-high tower isn't easy, it's still worth the trip. From its floor, you'll have a splendid view of the city. Because the town hall was torn down in 1820, this structure is now the only one standing on the square's western side. The climb to the top will also be an opportunity to explore Kraków's past, because a branch of the Museum of Kraków is located here. On the ground floor, you'll find a 15th-century parlour, which was used as a treasury during the Middle Ages. The first floor is where the councillors held meetings. The cellar, which was where the prison dungeons and torture chamber used to be, now houses a café and small theatre. *March–Nov Mon 11am–2.30pm, Tue–Sun 10am–5.30pm | admission 18 zł | Rynek Główny 1 | 🕮 c4*

6 KOŚCIÓŁ FRANCISZKANÓW (FRANCISCAN CHURCH) ★

The best time to visit this Gothic church is on sunny days. Originally consecrated in the 13th century, large parts of its current interior date back to the period when art nouveau was popular. Unfortunately, these parts are pretty dark, making it difficult to see the art. So it's best to choose a sunny day for your visit – you'll be able to see the art nouveau works by Stanisław Wyspiański under a much better light. He painted the walls with flowers and stars, and created the stained-glass windows for the presbytery as well as the one above the main entrance, called "Creation of the World". *Daily 6.30am–8pm except during trade fairs | Plac Wszystkich Świętych 5 | 🕮 b5*

7 COLLEGIUM MAIUS ★

Founded by King Kasimir the Great in 1364, Jagiellonian University is Poland's oldest academic institution and one of the oldest in the world. The Collegium Maius is the city's oldest university building. In the arcades around the Gothic inner courtyard, be sure to seek out the crystalline vaulting. The structure looks more like a monastery than a university.

The popular carillon happens every two hours *(9am, 11am, 1pm, 3pm, 5pm)*. It features a procession of clockwork historical figures and ends with the tune "Gaudeamus Igitur" ("So Let Us Rejoice"). If you miss it, you can get a feel for the 15th century – when Nicolaus Copernicus studied here – with a visit to the Gothic cellar café. A monument to the astronomer stood in the courtyard until the 1960s. Along with the future Pope John Paul II, he is one of the university's most famous students.

The University Museum is also well worth a visit. There are 30- and 70-minute tours that take you through the magnificent Gothic rooms of the library, the professors' dining room and the main lecture hall *(English tours available, times vary with season and length of tour, see website for booking). Admission from 17 zł, free Sat | Ulica Jagiellońska 15 | maius.uj.edu.pl | ⏲ 1–2 hr | 🕮 b4*

Not only is it Kraków's best example of late Baroque architecture, but it's also one of Poland's finest 18th-century buildings. It also has a beautiful *carillon (Mon–Sat 6.58am, 9am, noon, 3pm, 6pm, 9pm, Sun 7am, 9am, 11.48am, 3pm,*

INSIDER TIP
Best of Baroque

The Gothic exterior of the Franciscan Church hides its exuberant art nouveau interior

8 KOŚCIÓŁ ŚW. ANNY (ST ANNE'S CHURCH)

A church for academics. Since the early 18th century, students and professors of the nearby university have been coming to this elaborately decorated three-nave basilica. Artist Balthasar Fontana decorated the church with stucco and paintings. Each work attempts to create a sensation of three dimensionality and depth. Designed by court architect Tylman van Gameren, the church was completed in 1703.

6pm, 9pm). The church organ is also a feast for the eyes and ears. *Daily 8am–noon, 4–7pm | Ulica św. Anny 11 | kolegiata-anna.pl | 🕮 b3*

9 PLANTY

At Planty, fortress walls have been turned into a peaceful park. The 4km-long green belt that encircles the Old Town was placed where the medieval city walls and moats used to be. Take in the fresh air while strolling through the the park, which is laced with paths, and full of ponds, flower beds and meadows. It's a great way to experience the city's outdoors and see it from another angle. An added attraction is the collection of outdoor monuments from the 19th and 20th centuries. The park's sculptures are of great Polish artists, such as painter Artur Grottger. Other sculptures show fictional characters taken from Polish literature. You'll also find numerous benches with QR codes. Scan them with your smartphone to learn about the works of writers and poets, such as Stanisław Lem, Jerzy Pilch, Joseph Conrad, Georg Trakl and Herta Müller (see p. 26). The 20-hectare green area is perfect for joggers. *a–f 1–6*

INSIDER TIP
Run around the city

10 FORTIFICATIONS

Invaders must have had a really hard time trying to take over Kraków in the Middle Ages. To start with, the city was surrounded by a strengthened double wall 3m thick. If that wasn't enough, 47 fortified towers and a deep moat around the city also protected it from intruders. The guilds had the responsibility of protecting the bastions, where they also stored part of their arsenal of weapons. To top it off, the *Barbakane* (barbican), a round, fortified complex with seven slender turrets, was added in the 15th century. These measures kept the city safe for 400 years. However, as was the case for most major European cities, these medieval fortifications were demolished once protective walls and towers were deemed useless for defence.

What remains today is just a small section of the inner wall, two of its bastions, the arsenal, the barbican and the main entrance gate. The barbican and the walls are open to the public. Once you reach the higher floors, you'll have an interesting view over the city. A permanent exhibition

The Planty is both a green space and an open-air gallery surrounding the Old Town

shows the development and history of the complex, and further details are provided in two or three temporary shows every year. In summer, you'll find artists offering their work for sale inside the walls at Planty, and regular concerts and jousting also take place here. Leave the fortification complex through the main gate, the *Porta Gloriae*, to return to the city. This is where the Royal Route begins, and it opens up a spectacular view of the Ulica Floriańska with St Mary's Church and the Rynek Główny. *April–Oct Wed–Sun 10am–6pm | admission (Barbican and walls) 16 zł | entrance to the walls from Ulica Pijarska | e1–2*

SIDER TIP
Summer art at the walls

11 MUZEUM CZARTORYSKICH (CZARTORYSKI MUSEUM) ★

After reopening a few years ago, the country's oldest museum has once again been restored to its former splendour, with plenty of gold, glass and some hefty chandeliers. Tickets offer entry to the permanent exhibitions as well as a small temporary exhibition that changes every three months. The museum displays prints and books from the Czartoryski Library.

For many, however, the standout piece is Leonardo da Vinci's *Lady with an Ermine.* Leave plenty of time if you plan to visit the *Mona Lisa*'s lesser-known sister on the second floor of the museum's gallery: there is usually a queue! Still, it's worth the wait, with many who have already seen the portrait of Cecilia Gallerani, mistress to the Duke of Milan Lodovico Sforza, claiming this lady is even more enchanting than her Parisian counterpart with the famously enigmatic smile.

The museum dates back to 1786, when it was founded by Princess Izabela Czartoryska. Her intention was not just to collect art but to preserve the memory of the greats of Polish history. As a result, this patriotic part of the collection can prove a little tedious for those who aren't experts on Polish history.

Nonetheless, there is also the aforementioned second floor, which houses one of the most valuable art collections in Europe. Here, Rembrandt's *Landscape with the Good Samaritan* hangs alongside the Da Vinci and countless other marvellous paintings and sculptures, as well as jewellery, Egyptian art and works from the Far East.

Overwhelmed by so much beauty? Sit back and absorb everything you have just seen in the palace's beautiful glass-roofed courtyard over cake and nibbles in the café. We recommend the excellent audio guide *(10 zł)* to take you through the exhibition. Numbered tickets are valid for a specific time and you can buy them online from 31 days before your visit, with a limited number available at the ticket desk. *Tue–Sun 10am–6pm | admission 60 zł, Tue free (tickets at the counter) | Ulica Pijarska 15 | mnk.pl/branch/mnk-czartoryski-museum | 2-3 hrs | d2*

INSIDER TIP
Knowledge in your ear

12 POLONIA WAX MUSEUM

When Scrat, the acorn-driven, sabre-toothed squirrel from *Ice Age*, Spiderman and the Joker are all in one room, it's either the start of a joke or you've made it to the Polonia Wax Museum. The kids may not enjoy seeing John Paul II and the other Polish celebrities, but what about Harry and Hermione, or William and Kate? *Daily 9am–10pm | admission 50 zł, children 40 zł | Ulica Floriańska 32 | poloniawaxmuseum.com | 1 Std | d2*

13 TEATR SŁOWACKIEGO (SŁOWACKI THEATRE)

First Vienna and then Kraków – having first opened in 1893, this is the city's most beautiful theatre. It boasts a variety of styles and motifs in its neo-Baroque architecture, similar to other theatres built under the Habsburg Empire. It's also like a miniature version of the Paris Opéra Garnier. Although the performances are only in Polish, you really shouldn't miss seeing the interior's extravagant splendour. The original main curtain is one of the theatre's many highlights, as it's raised off the ground rather than rolled up. The allegorical scene shown on the front is a personification of artistic inspiration, comedy and tragedy. *Plac Świętego Ducha 1 | slowacki.krakow.pl | e2*

14 MUZEUM FARMACJI (PHARMACY MUSEUM)

If you've ever wondered how dragon blood is used in medicine, you'll find the answer here. This museum's design is that of an old pharmacy. From the cellar up to the attic, you'll find remedies both bizarre and pharmaceutically useful and gain some interesting insight into the history of

The faithful are welcomed to St Peter & St Paul's Church by the twelve apostles

medicine since the Middle Ages. Marvel at old scales, stuffed exotic animals, amulets, poisons, medical musk products and minerals. Dried bats hang from the ceiling, and there's a room full of herbs in the attic. *Tue noon–6.30pm, Wed–Sat 9.30am–3pm | admission 14 zł | Ulica Floriańska 25 | muzeumfarmacji.uj.edu.pl | ⏱ 1 hr | 🗺 d3*

SOUTHERN OLD TOWN

A fire-breathing dragon and a castle full of treasure! The silhouettes of the Wawel Cathedral and the Royal Castle – highlights of the Kraków cityscape – promise plenty of exciting and impressive stories for history fans to discover at closer quarters.

Before you make your way up the hill you should take a closer look at the bishops' palaces on Ulica Kanonicza. Although remnants of Pope John Paul II are seen all over Kraków, they are especially common here. Karol Wojtyła lived on Ulica Kanonicza while he was a bishop and archbishop, and worked in the Wawel Cathedral on the hill.

15 KOŚCIÓŁ ŚW. PIOTRA I PAWŁA (ST PETER & ST PAUL'S CHURCH)

This church enables visitors to see the earth's rotation up close. You can witness this phenomenon when the church lowers a Foucault's pendulum from the ceiling. The pendulum's swing proves that the earth rotates *(demonstrations Thur 10am, 11am, noon)*. This single-nave church in red brick and light-coloured granite was Poland's first Baroque church. Construction started in 1597 and lasted until 1619 due to problems with the dome. It is an exact copy of the Jesuit Church of the Gesù in Rome – some people go so far as to say that the proportions in Kraków are even better than those of the church it was modelled on.

INSIDER TIP **Swing of the pendulum**

The church often puts on summer concerts; check the posters at the entrance for information. The building is also cold, even in summer, so don't forget your pullover if you attend a performance. *April–Oct Tue–Sat 9am–5pm, Sun 1.30–5pm, Nov–March Tue–Sat 11am–3pm, Sun 1.30–5pm, except during services | Ulica Grodzka 52a | apostolowie.pl | 🗺 D7*

INSIDER TIP **Summer chill**

16 KOŚCIÓŁ ŚW. ANDRZEJA (ST ANDREW'S CHURCH)

Don't let the church's austere exterior put you off. With its Romanesque style and unique double towers, it's actually one of the city's oldest. Dating back to the 11th century, this fortified church is equipped with embrasures and walls up to 1.6m thick. These defences were often used to protect the city's people, including in 1241, when the Mongols ran riot through Kraków. The interior of the small, three-nave church is even more beautiful. It boasts an altar made of black marble and a ship-shaped pulpit. The sight of this Baroque golden structure will leave you in awe. *Daily 7am–6pm | Ulica Grodzka 54 | klaryski.pl | D8*

17 ULICA KANONICZA (KANONICZA STREET)

Each of the buildings on this narrow road is worth observing. This is the last section of the Royal Route leading to the castle, and a lot goes on here. It's well worth your time to take a walk past the illuminated buildings here on a warm evening. The street is named after the people who lived on it. The canons of the cathedral chapter were the bishops' advisers and built their palaces here, at the foot of the hill. The façades and richly decorated portals of the houses at numbers 1, 3, 9, 13 and 15 are especially interesting. Behind their Gothic façades, you'll often find Renaissance arcaded courtyards reminiscent of the Royal Castle. *C7–8*

18 MUZEUM ERAZMA CIOŁKA (ERAZM CIOŁEK MUSEUM)

One of the National Museum's many branches. Inside the palace you'll find priceless 14th- to 16th-century paintings and sculptures in its *Art of Old Poland* collection. These include a large number of Gothic altarpieces. The hall, which is devoted to Baroque Polish funerary art, is particularly impressive. Religious music plays in the background and various coffins and pictures of coffins are on display. You'll also come across *Orthodox Art of the Old Republic*, which shows icons and objects used in the liturgy of the Eastern Church. The Orthodox icons are part of one of the oldest and most valuable collections in central Europe. Below, in the beautifully restored cellar, is a collection of sculptures and decorative elements taken from important architectural sites in Poland. The music comes from a stone instrument called a lithophone. *Tue 10am–6pm, Wed–Sun 10am–4pm | admission 18 zł, audio guide 7 zł, Tue free | Ulica Kanonicza 17 | mnk.pl/branch/mnk-the-ciolek | 1 hr | C8*

19 MUZEUM PRZYRODNICZE PAN (NATURAL HISTORY MUSEUM)

Marvel at various snakes, lizards, turtles, and frogs. See tropical fish in their own coral reef and be dazzled by luminescent creatures from the depths of the ocean. There's even a 30,000-year-old preserved woolly rhinoceros on display, which was discovered in the Ukrainian village of Starunia. *Tue–Fri 9am–3pm, Sat noon–6pm | 25 zł, children 18 zł | Ulica św. Sebastiana 9 | isez.pan.krakow.pl/muzeum.html | 1 hr | D8*

20 KATEDRA ŚW. STANISŁAWA I ŚW. WACŁAWA (WAWEL CATHEDRAL)

Are those really the bones of the Wawel Dragon hanging up to the left of the entrance? Or are they those of a whale, mammoth or rhino? Either way, they serve an important purpose: on the day they fall to the ground, we'll

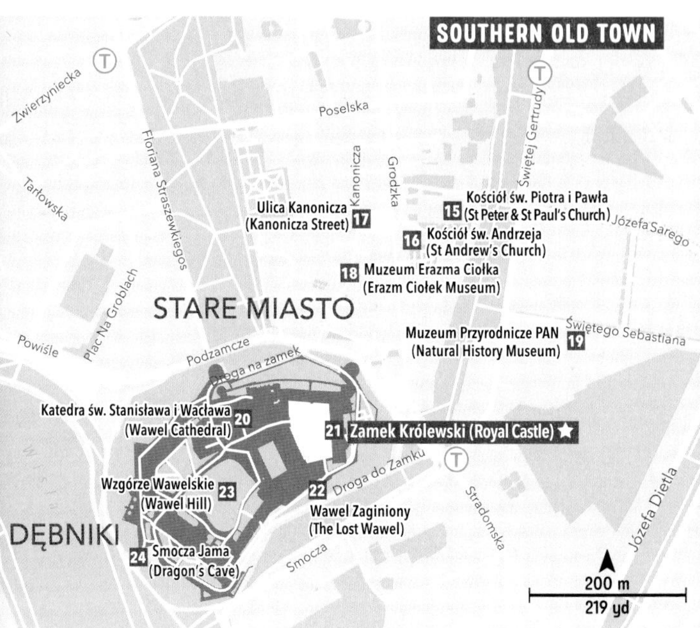

know the world is coming to an end. Unfortunately, we still don't have enough evidence to prove whether this legend is true. What we do know is that the Cathedral of St Stanislaus and St Wenceslaus, as Kraków's cathedral is officially known (Wavel Cathedral is its more commonly used name), stands on Wawel Hill, close to the castle, and is hands down the most important church in all of Poland on account of its symbolic meaning and function. It is on this site that Poland's kings were crowned. The current building is actually the third church to occupy the space. Construction began in the 14th century and the cathedral was altered countless times over the centuries; it now combines architectural styles from Gothic to modern. Poland's kings were buried here too, and the cathedral houses a large number of royal coffins. President Lech Kaczyński and his wife, who both perished in a plane crash in April 2010, were also laid to rest in its crypt.

The three-nave basilica is flanked by two Gothic chapels. The one on the right, seen from the entrance, the *Holy Cross Chapel*, is especially noteworthy. It was decorated with Russian-Byzantine frescoes in the 15th century and is also the site of the marble grave Veit Stoss created for King Kazimierz Jegiellończyk. A Baroque silver sarcophagus with the relics of St Stanisław occupies a central place in the cathedral.

The cathedral itself is rather small for a royal church, but it does include a large number of other chapels. Two are particularly notable: the *Kaplica Zygmuntowska (Sigismund Chapel)* and the *Kaplica Wazów (Waza Chapel)*. The first has been described as the "pearl of the Renaissance north of the Alps". The purity of its style and perfect symmetry is still admired today. It was created out of red Hungarian marble, combined with white stone, by the Italian master Bartolommeo Berrecci in the 16th century. The Waza Chapel represents the zenith of Baroque art and design and is decorated with black marble.

The cathedral's front door is decorated with bones to remind visitors of the transience of life.

While you're here, you should definitely visit the *Wieża Zygmuntowska (Sigismund Tower)*, with its fabulous panoramic view. The bell at the top shares the tower's name and is the largest in Poland. It has a diameter of 2.5m and weighs 12 tons. According to legend, all those who touch the bell are guaranteed eternal love and happiness for the rest of their days.

On display in the *Cathedral Museum* are objects associated with Pope John Paul II, which have been taken from the treasury for display here. They include chalices, monstrances and garments. Photography is prohibited in the museum. *April–Oct Mon–Sat 9am–5pm, Sun 12.30–5pm, Nov–March until 4pm, Cathedral Museum closed Sun | admission to main nave, royal tombs, Sigismund Tower, various chapels, the Cathedral Museum and Museum of the Archdiocese (Tue–Sun 10am–5pm | Ulica Kanonicza 19) 23 zł, audio guide 13 zł | Wawel 3 | katedra-wawelska.pl | ⊞ C8*

Poland's kings were crowned and buried in Wawel Cathedral

21 ZAMEK KRÓLEWSKI (ROYAL CASTLE) ★

Since it was originally built in the 11th century, the Royal Castle has caught fire so many times that you'd think matches would be banned by now. It was, after all, a fire that led King Zygmunt Stary to have the castle reconstructed in Renaissance style (1504–1536). Italian artists from Florence created the monumental three-storey building, with its beautifully arcaded inner courtyard. It was the official residence of Poland's monarchs until the end of the 16th century – that is until the building caught fire again. In response, King Zygmunt III Vaza and his court moved to Warsaw. This time, the castle was reconstructed in Baroque style, but only served as the royals' weekend residence. Over the years, many others occupied, plundered and renovated it.

Today, there's a museum in the castle, and each room is open to the public. Among the many treasures is a collection of 16th-century tapestries said to be some of the most beautiful in the world. King Zygmunt August commissioned them to be made in Brussels, using wool, gold and silver thread, and silk. They were made to measure for the rooms and originally covered most of the walls; they recount three of the most important stories from the Bible: Adam and Eve, the Tower of Babel, and Noah's Ark. *Reprezentacyjne komnaty królewskie (State Rooms): opening hours change seasonally; see website | admission 35 zł, with guided tour 55 zł, online ticket 36 zł. Prywatne komnaty królewskie (Royal Private Apartments): as above | admission 30 zł.*

The crown jewels are on the ground floor of the oldest section of the castle. Here, you'll see the Gothic remains of its earlier structure and, more importantly, the *Szczerbiec* – the coronation sword of the Polish kings. Weapons from the 15th to 19th centuries, as well as medieval armour, are on display in the nearby armoury. *Skarbiec Koronny i Zbrojownia (Crown Treasury and Armoury): opening hours change seasonally; see website | admission Crown Treasury 35 zł, Armoury 20 zł, free admission Mon but entry is still ticketed.*

Your best bet is to buy tickets online at least one week in advance. You can also buy tickets on site either at the entrance gate *(Brama Herbowa | May–Oct Mon 9am–3.20pm, Tue–Sun 9am–4.20pm)* or at the Information Centre *(Centrum Promocji i Informacji | daily 9am–5pm, tickets Mon 9am–3.20pm, Tue–Sun 9am–4.20pm)*. Expect long queues during the high season. Tickets are limited and only valid for specific time slots. You can avoid the queues by coming early. You'll also find toilets *(2 zł)*, souvenir shops, a post office, restaurants and cafés at the information centre. Note that photography is prohibited inside the castle. Rucksacks must be left in the cloakroom, and visitors are not permitted to carry sharp objects (pocket knives, nail files, and so on). In summer, you'll have a lovely view from the terrace at *Café Słodki Wawel*.

INSIDER TIP
Summer views

Castle: Mon 10am–4pm, Jan–March Tue–Fri 9.30am–5pm, April–June, Sept–Dec Tue–Fri 9am–5pm, July/Aug Tue–Fri 9am–6pm | Wawel 5 | wawel.krakow.pl | 2–3 hrs | C8

22 WAWEL ZAGINIONY (THE LOST WAWEL)

What did Wawel Hill look like from the 10th to 14th centuries? Travel back in time with the help of models, films and an almost completely preserved early Romanesque rotunda from the 10th or 11th century. *Opening hours change seasonally, see website | admission 15 zł, Mon free admission | Wawel 5 | wawel.krakow.pl | 30 mins | C8*

23 WZGÓRZE WAWELSKIE (WAWEL HILL)

Wawel Hill offers one of the best views of the city – a sight most likely first enjoyed by people living here during the Palaeolithic Age. This assumption is based on the fact that archaeologists have found proof of people settling here long before the areas around Kraków were Christianised in the tenth century. The fact that the hill not only had fresh spring water but was also surrounded by the Vistula on all sides made it a strategically ideal location. Today, it is no longer possible to see where the Vistula originally flowed because the river was diverted in the 19th century and is now Ulica Dietla, one of the loveliest and busiest streets in Kraków. *Summer until 9pm | free admission | no bicycles or dogs | C8–9*

24 SMOCZA JAMA (DRAGON'S CAVE)

Luckily, the story of the virgin-eating dragon who lived in a cave ends with the beast's demise. Although it's just a legend, there is a possibility that the tale contains a kernel of truth, as archaeologists have found bones of prehistoric animals in the cave, which is around 11m years old. The Dragon's Cave is entered from the top of the Wawel Hill and exited at the Vistula. The path is illuminated in such a way that the mythical figure could be around any corner. And then – bam! – there he is – standing at the exit in the form of a fire-breathing *metal sculpture*! *End April–Aug daily 10.30am–7pm, Sept/Oct until 6pm | admission 9 zł, children 7 zł | Wawel 5 | wawel.krakow.pl | 30 mins | C9*

KAZIMIERZ

Cafés, pubs, clubs and artists: Kazimierz is popular for its bohemian charm, but its (often tragic) Jewish history has not been forgotten.

This hip district is walking distance from the city centre and a popular spot to hang out for partygoers and night owls. At Plac Nowy, the heart of the district, you'll find plenty of cafés, pubs and clubs that stay open late (until the early hours, to be more specific) in summer. Kazimierz is especially enjoyable in the evening, with its klezmer concerts and Jewish restaurants along Ulica Szeroka.

What is now a much-loved district was an independent town until the 19th century, with a marketplace, town hall and many magnificent monasteries. Rich in Jewish history, the Jews who came here from Kraków in the 15th century had their homes in an enclosed section around Ulica Szeroka. It was home to seven synagogues, plus cemeteries, businesses and schools. Everything was peaceful until 1941, when the Nazi occupiers deported the Jews to the ghetto in the Podgórze district of Kraków.

Life changed after that, and Kazimierz came to a standstill – that is, until Steven Spielberg came to shoot his film *Schindler's List* here. The tourists soon followed, and once again the area was buzzing. Its Jewish history was present again, but this time with painful memories of suffering.

You can walk to Kazimierz from the city centre *(15 mins from Wawel Hill via Ulica Stradom and Ulica Krakówska, or from Poczta Główna via Ulica Starowiślna)*. You can also travel here by tram *(nos. 3, 6, 8, 13 from Wawel to Plac Wolnica or 24 from Poczta Główna to Miodowa)*.

Jewish traditions live on in Kazimierz's restaurants

25 PLAC NOWY (NEW SQUARE)

There are plenty of restaurants, hip clubs and landmark pubs to visit here, including *Alchemia* (see p. 85), where guests enjoy sitting at tables outdoors in summer. Revellers flood Plac Nowy, the district's square, and it's particularly popular with young people. What makes the square really special, though, is that it still retains its historical function. Today, although the goods sold here have changed, the square is still a place for trade.

INSIDER TIP
Stop for a snack!

The Okrąglak food hall, for example, was a kosher poultry abattoir until 1939. Today, they sell delicious *zapiekanki* at small snack bars. This cult snack costs somewhere between 15 and 20 zł and is a kind of Polish pizza. The most popular stand is the *U Endziora*, but you'll have to queue.

A food and flower market is held on the Plac Nowy daily, and there is a flea market at weekends. Here, you'll find clothing, bags and jewellery (including designer articles at excellent prices). On Saturdays, antiques like Jewish silverware can be found. *E9*

26 SYNAGOGA REMUH (REMUH SYNAGOGUE)

The seven synagogues in Kazimierz have all been preserved, and regular services are still held in the renovated 16th-century Remuh Synagogue on the Sabbath (after sunset on Friday and on Saturday) and other Jewish holidays. Morning prayers also take place here. The interior is very simple and tastefully decorated, in keeping with a Torah commandment not to use decorations from the living world in art. The traditional division into separate sections for men and women is discernible in the synagogue's architecture.

The neighbouring *Old Jewish Cemetery (Stary Cmentarz)* is no longer in use but is well worth visiting to see its many old gravestones. The largest tomb is that of Moses Isserles Remuh, a well-known rabbi from the 16th century. Today, Jews from all over the world make pilgrimages to his grave.

You will see remnants of *macevas* (Jewish gravestones) that were found during renovation work in the 1950s on the eastern wall to the right of the entrance to the cemetery. The locals

The Old Synagogue is simple, beautiful and 600 years old

call it the "Wailing Wall" after its counterpart in Jerusalem. Men have to cover their head if they want to visit the synagogue or cemetery – if you do not have a cap with you, you can borrow a *kippah* free of charge in the synagogue. *Daily 10am–6pm, until 4pm in winter | admission 10 zł | Ulica Szeroka 40 | gwzkrakow.pl | ⏲ 30 mins | 🕮 E9*

27 SYNAGOGA STARA (OLD SYNAGOGUE)

Rebuilt during the Renaissance, this old Gothic synagogue now houses a Jewish cultural museum. The museum tells the story of everyday Jewish life: knives used for slaughtering animals in accordance with Jewish laws, circumcision instruments, crowns and bells for the Torah. The temple dates from the end of the 15th century and is the oldest synagogue in Poland. You will notice the traditional separation into different sections for men and women even before you enter. *Mon 10am–2pm, Tue–Sun 10am–5pm | admission 18 zł, free Mon | Ulica Szeroka 24 | short.travel/kra15 | ⏲ 30 mins | 🕮 F9*

28 MUZEUM GALICIA (GALICIA JEWISH MUSEUM)

This private museum is devoted to paying tribute to Holocaust victims. The exhibition "Traces of Memory" depicts the history of Jewish life in the Galicia region, within which Kraków is located, and is exceptionally well documented. The photos on display were taken by photographer Chris Schwarz. His pictures take visitors on a journey through the eastern regions of modern-day Poland and Ukraine. Inside, you'll also find a café and well-stocked bookstore that offers plenty of literature on Galicia and Jewish history. Visit the website for more information.

Daily 10am–6pm | admission 20 zł | Ulica Dajwór 18 | galiciajewish museum.org | ⏲ 1 hr | 🕮 F9

29 KOŚCIÓŁ BOŻEGO CIAŁA (CORPUS CHRISTI CHURCH) ★

The parish church in Kazimierz, on the former marketplace, is one of the city's most beautiful Gothic churches. Legend has it that when it was built, people saw a strange light for weeks above the construction site. The workers digging here also discovered a monstrance that had disappeared from a church in Kraków. Particularly worth seeing in this monumental church dating back to 1340 are its main altar and boat-shaped pulpit. *Daily 6am–8pm, except during services | Ulica Bożego Ciała 26 | bozecialo.net | 🕮 E10*

Next door is the *Mużeum Inzynierii i Techniki (Tue–Sun 10am–6pm | admission 35 zl, children (3–6) 10 zl | Świętego Wawrzyńca 15 | mit.krakow),* located in a former tram depot. The museum has fascinating exhibitions on engineering (particularly transport) and technology.

The Botanical Gardens provide a peaceful oasis of green

30 KOŚCIÓŁ PAULINÓW NA SKAŁCE (PAULINE CHURCH ON THE ROCK)

Legend has it that St Stanisław, the country's most important patron saint, was beheaded where this 18th-century Baroque church now stands and his body was thrown into the nearby well. People claim its water took on healing powers, making the well a place of pilgrimage. A procession in honour of St Stanisław is organised every year in May – it begins at the cathedral and ends at this three-nave basilica, with its magnificent black marble portal. *Daily 6am–8pm, except during services | Ulica Skałeczna 15 | skalka.paulini.pl | 🕮 C10*

OTHER DISTRICTS

31 OGRÓD BOTANICZNY (BOTANICAL GARDENS)

The most beautiful seasons in the Botanical Gardens are summer and early autumn, when the lilies, peonies and irises are in full bloom. The former observatory now houses the *Botanical Garden Museum*, including the largest collection of orchids in Poland. The oldest tree in the gardens is a 500-year-old oak. *Open hours change seasonally, see website | admission 15 zł | Ulica Kopernika 27 | ogrod.uj.edu.pl | G–H5–6*

32 ULICA POMORSKA (POMORSKA STREET)

During World War II, this building was the headquarters of the Gestapo. Now, the moving exhibition here not only traces the history of the Nazis' reign of terror, but also of the Great Purge during the Soviet era. In the former Gestapo cells, you'll find more than 600 words, prayers and pleas that were etched into the walls by prisoners. *Wed–Sun 10am–5pm | admission 16 zł, Wed free, combined ticket with the Memory Trail 45 zł* *(see p. 53) | Ulica Pomorska 2 | muzeumkrakow.pl/en/branches/pomorska-street | 1 hr | A3*

33 DOM MEHOFFERA (JÓZEF MEHOFFER HOUSE)

At this house museum, filled with original furnishings, family photos and souvenirs, you'll feel as if you're in the home of one of Poland's greatest art nouveau painters: Józef Mehoffer (1869–1946). In 1932, Mehoffer bought the house where Stanisław Wyspiański was born, a neoclassical villa in Nowy Świat. This is where he and his family lived until his death. On display are his paintings and other projects, such as the stained-glass windows he designed for Freiburg Cathedral. The garden next to the house is an oasis of greenery right in the middle of the city and perfect for a break from sightseeing. *Tue 10am–6pm, Wed–Sun 10am–4pm, garden and Café Ważka 10am–9.30pm | admission 18 zł, Tue free | Ulica Krupnicza 26 | mnk.pl/branch/mnk-the-mehoffer | 1 hr | B5*

INSIDER TIP
Take a break in the garden

34 MUZEUM WYSPIAŃSKI

Another branch of the National Museum, this time located in a 17th-century warehouse that has been renovated in exemplary fashion. Until recently, the building housed the Europeum European Cultural Centre, but the focus now falls on the life and art of Stanisław Wyspianski, the most famous artist of the Polish art nouveau movement and a key member of the Młoda Polska (Young Poland) movement. The artist lived and died in Kraków, experimenting with painting, illustrating, playwriting and designing stained-glass windows. He became a veritable 19th-century Renaissance figure and a true Kraków icon. A beautiful courtyard complete with deckchairs and parasols is a great spot to take a break. *Tue, Fri–Sun 10am–5pm | admission 18 zł, Tue free | Plac Sikorskiego 6 | mnk.pl/branch/mnk-wyspianski | 1 hr | B6*

35 MUZEUM NARODOWE (NATIONAL MUSEUM)

Founded in 1879, the National Museum's holdings grew so quickly that it became necessary to move some of its departments to other locations. These include the picture gallery in *Cloth Hall*, the *Czartoryski*, *Erazma Ciołka* and *Wyspiański* museums, and the *Józef Mehoffer House*. You can buy a combined ticket for 120 zł that entitles you to entry into all branches of the National Museum (with the exception of the Czartoryski Museum). The most interesting sections in this, the main building, are the military exhibition, a collection of Polish arts and crafts and the *Gallery of 20th-Century Polish Art*, which is particularly good. The museum also houses a new shop and a café. *Tue–Sun 10am–6pm | admission 32 zł, Tue free, audio-guide 7 zł | Aleja 3 Maja 1 | mnk.pl/branch/mnk-the-main-building | 1–2 hrs | A6*

36 MUZEUM WITRAZU (STAINED-GLASS MUSEUM)

If you liked the stained glass windows in the cathedral and Franciscan Church, you'll be interested to know they were made in the Zelenski family's workshop, now home to this museum. Not only can you see the glass on display here, but you can also watch the windows being made. Take a two two- to three-hour to three-hour course and make your own glass object. A stylish café and small souvenir shop are also on the premises. *Guided tours only (in English) Tue–Sat noon, 3pm, online reservations recommended | admission 50 zł, courses start at 250 zł | Aleja Krasinskiego 23 | muzeumwitrazu.pl | 1 hr | A7*

37 CRICOTEKA

If you're looking at an old power station beneath a massive steel structure, you've made it to the Centre of Documentation of the Art of Tadeusz Kantor (1915–1990). Together with his experimental theatre group Cricot 2, this theatre director, painter, performance artist, set designer, writer and actor achieved European acclaim for his play *Dead Class*, a work that broke down conventional boundaries between the visual arts and theatre. The structure also offers a bookshop, a café and an unparalleled view of the city from the top floor. *Tue–Sun 11am–7pm | Ulica Nadwiślańska 2–4 | admission free | news.cricoteka.pl | 1 hr | F10–11*

38 MOCAK MUZEUM SZTUKI WSPÓŁCZESNEJ W KRAKÓWIE (MUSEUM OF CONTEMPORARY ART)

At the Museum of Contemporary Art (MOCAK), you'll find the latest trends in modern art, both from Poland and worldwide. It offers a permanent exhibition alongside interesting temporary shows. Parts of the Schindler Factory were used to construct the

The Museum of Contemporary Art is a colourful contrast to Kraków's ever-present history

museum. *Tue–Sun 11am–7pm | admission 25 zł, free Thur | Ulica Lipowa 4 | mocak.pl | Tram 3, 9, 11, 20,49, 50, 72 Zabłocie | 1–2 hrs | H10*

39 FABRYKA SCHINDLERA (SCHINDLER FACTORY) ★

The Museum of the City of Kraków established the permanent exhibition on the fate of its Jewish and non-Jewish citizens, "Kraków under Nazi Occupation 1939–1945" on the premises of *Oskar Schindler's Enamel Factory*. On the three floors of the museum, visitors can get a taste of what life was like for the people living in Kraków during the Nazi occupation. You'll learn about the horrible conditions in the ghetto and the long-awaited liberation of the city by the Red Army in January 1945. The factory's office has been preserved in its original state in memory of Oskar Schindler, who produced enamelware and later ammunition for the German army in his factory. Although Schindler was originally only interested in making money, he decided to save more than 1,100 Jews after the Nazis liquidated the ghetto in March 1943 by pretending they were needed to produce materials essential to the war effort. Schindler's actions became world famous with the release Steven Spielberg's film *Schindler's List* in 1993. The Schindler Factory is included in the *Memory Trail (muzeumkrakowa.pl/en, combined ticket 47 zł)*, along with the *Eagle Pharmacy* (see p. 54) and *Ulica Pomorska* (see p. 51), the Gestapo prison. *Mon 10am–2pm, Tue–Sat 9am–6pm, closed 1st Tue of month | admission 32 zł, free Mon (come early!), book tickets online if possible, only recommended for children 14 and older | Ulica Lipowa 4 | short.travel/*

kra16 | tram 1, 3, 5, 17, 19, 24, 69 Plac Bohaterów Getta | ⏲ 2 hrs | 🕮 H10

40 PODGÓRZE

In March 1941, the Nazis set up a Jewish ghetto within a section of the Podgórze suburb. Some 16,000 people were forced to live where only 3,000 had made their homes previously – in unbelievably cramped conditions. Today, there is no wall or plaque to show where the ghetto was. Instead, an installation of metal chairs on *Plac Bohaterów Getta (Ghetto Heroes Square)* recalls the ghetto's destruction in March 1943, when all of the furniture and personal belongings of the people living there were simply thrown out of their windows. The inhabitants were then either shot or transported to concentration camps.

Close by is the *Apteka Pod Orłem* or *Eagle Pharmacy (Wed–Sun 10am–5pm | admission 18 zł,* 🐷 *free Wed | Plac Bohaterów Getta 18 | short.travel/kra17l)*, the only one to supply medicine to the Jews living in the ghetto. Many, mostly children, were saved by Catholic pharmacist Tadeusz Pankiewicz, who hid them from the Nazi thugs in the cupboards in his shop. Today, the pharmacy houses a museum. The highly informative, interactive exhibition has been revamped in recent years and is well worth a visit. It tells the history of the ghetto and the people who tried to survive there, focusing on the pharmacy as a place of refuge. *Tram 1, 3, 5, 17, 19, 24, 69 Plac Bohaterów Getta | 🕮 d–f 9–10*

41 NOWA HUTA

Visiting Nowa Huta is like entering another world and is an exciting and rewarding trip. It takes a while to get there, so plan at least half a day for your visit. This district of Kraków was built from the ground up in 1949 under Russian occupation. The Russians wanted to build a model communist city with a complete infrastructure, wide streets and many parks. Its inhabitants, who were transported en masse from rural parts of Poland, were given flats of modern design in concrete blocks to live in. The government also gave them a job at the Vladimir Lenin Steelworks, which was conveniently located next door.

The experiment ultimately failed because residents rejected the whole concept behind Nowa Huta, which had been built partly to act as a counterweight to Kraków's liberal intellectual culture. Many residents who had grown up in the countryside refused to adopt the way of life prescribed by its communist creators. Instead, they preferred to continue their earlier life, farming livestock (sometimes from the comfort of their own balcony!) and attending church regularly.

Churchgoers put Nowa Huta on the map with its *Ark of the Lord Church (daily 6.30am–6pm, except during services | Ulica Obrońców Krzyża 1 | arkapana.pl | bus 139 Arka)*, the first in this communist model community. Residents fought for more than ten years to get permission to build the church and many paid with their lives in the protests that took place. After an

The striking Jesus statue in the Ark of the Lord Church, Nowa Huta

additional ten years of construction, it was finally consecrated by the then archbishop, Karol Wojtyła, in 1977.

Its modern architecture reminds one of Le Corbusier's famous chapel in Ronchamp. The Nowa Huta church is shaped like a large boat with the cross as its mast. The most impressive features of the interior are the wooden roof construction and enormous bronze sculpture of the crucified Christ that stretches from floor to ceiling. The tabernacle contains a crystal that the crew of Apollo 11 brought back from the moon.

The most interesting architecture in Nowa Huta comes from the 1950s and 1960s and can be seen on *Plac Centralny (Central Square)*, the starting point for the four main roads and a pedestrian avenue *(Aleja Róż)*. Influenced by neoclassicism, the buildings consist of large and sunny apartments, and there are spacious parks nearby. The architecture from the later phase (1970s and 1980s) is completely different. Built quickly and cheaply, high, grey Soviet-style blocks of flats – with a planned 8m² per person – set the tone in this section of the district.

To this day, it has not been possible to merge Nowa Huta and the 250,000 people living here with the other districts of Kraków – the differences in culture and social structure are simply too great. In addition, the workers' district is now struggling with unemployment. After the steelworks were privatised, many of the workers were made redundant. *Tram 1 Teatr Ludowy, 4 Plac Centralny, 15 Cystesów, bus 139 Arka* | *e–f 8–9*

DAY TRIPS

42 OGRÓD ZOOLOGICZNY (ZOOLOGICAL GARDENS)

8km / 20 mins by car

Built in 1927 and one of Poland's oldest zoos. More than 1,500 animals, including 32 endangered species, live on this 20-hectare site in the beautiful Wolski Forest, which is well worth the trip in itself. In May, the azaleas and rhododendrons are in full bloom. *Daily, opening hours change seasonally | 40 zł, children 34 zł | Ulica Kasy Oszczędności Miasta Krakowa 14 | zoo-krakow.pl | bus 134 Hotel Cracovia | 2 hrs | b9*

INSIDER TIP
Zoo in the woods

43 KOPALNIA SOLI WIELICZKA (WIELICZKA SALT MINES)

14km / 40 mins by train

The salt mines in Wieliczka are one of the main attractions in the environs of Kraków and have been a UNESCO World Heritage Site since 1978. From the 13th century onwards, the mines were one of the most important sources of revenue for Kraków and the entire kingdom; in its heyday in the 15th century, the salt trade accounted for more than 30% of the town's total revenue. Mining continued until well into the 20th century, but today very little salt is extracted.

There are more than 30km of labyrinthine paths on nine underground levels. The main attraction on the "Tourist Route" – in addition to the 20m-high chambers and a salt lake – is the *Kaplica św. Kingi (Chapel of St Kinga)*, where everything down to the chandelier, altars and floor is made of pure salt. The graduation tower *(admission 9 zł, combination ticket 6 zł)* offers a great view from its observation platform. Underground, the temperature is only 14° celsius, so don't forget your pullover! Buy tickets online or at the ticket office on site. To get here, travel from Kraków Głowny (Main) station to Wieliczka Rynek Kopalnia station. From here you can walk to the mine in a few minutes. *Opening hours change seasonally, see website | admission (only with tour, English tours available) starts at 122 zł depending on the season | Ulica Daniłowicza 10 | Wieliczka | wieliczka-saltmine.com f12*

44 AUSCHWITZ-BIRKENAU ★

70km / approx. 1½ hrs by car or bus

No other name evokes more images of the unimaginably horrific deeds perpetrated by the Nazis than that of the Auschwitz-Birkenau concentration camp. More than 1.2 million people – mostly Jews – were murdered in this, the largest German extermination camp. Today, there is a memorial site and museum on the 190-hectare site near Oświęcim (about 45km from Kraków). The organisation of what was originally a labour camp shows how the Nazis went about their work with perfidious technocratic coldness: the prisoners in Camp III (Monowitz) had to labour in the factories of the Buna Werke (IG Farben), while those in Auschwitz I were forced to build roads and houses. The largest section of the camp was where the barracks, prison, death cells, administration and the home of the camp's commanders – among them Rudolf Höss, who lived here with his family – were located. You can still see the cynical sign "Arbeit macht frei" ("Work sets you free") above the main gate to Auschwitz I.

The real horror took place in Auschwitz II (Birkenau): people were murdered in four large gas chambers and then incinerated in the crematoria. A visit to Auschwitz is a highly emotional – and shocking – experience; make sure that you, and particularly any children you may be with, are well prepared for what you will encounter. Plan about five hours for your visit. There's a free shuttle bus between the camps. Tickets must be bought online at *visit.auschwitz.org*. The free tickets are individual and assigned a number. Due to the high demand, it's best to book online (at least one month in advance). You could also book an organised tour from Kraków *(approx. 120 zł)* with, for example, *Cracow City Tours (see p. 118)*. Only small bags are allowed on site. *Daily Dec 7.30am–2pm, Jan, Nov 7.30am–3pm, Feb 7.30am–4pm, March, Oct 7.30am–5pm, April, May, Sept 7.30am–6pm, June–Aug 7.30am–7pm (you may stay up to 90 minutes after closing time). Visits are possible with or without a guide; without a guide only in the afternoon from 4pm | book an English tour at visit.auschwitz.org | guided tour from 100 zł, private guided tour from 150 zł, free without tour | Więźniów Oświęcimia 20 | Oświęcim | auschwitz.org/en. Getting there: minibuses from Kraków railway station or by car via Dw 780, Dk 44 or A4 towards Oświecim, follow the signs for Muzeum Auschwitz | ◫ 0*

Everything is made from salt in the Chapel of St Kinga

EATING & DRINKING

Kraków offers excellent Polish cooking, but the international cuisine from many other countries is also superb. Food here is anything but bland!

Even during communist times, Kraków had a great culinary reputation. And while you may pay slightly higher prices than elsewhere in Poland, dishes are still far more modestly priced than in many other European tourist hotspots.

Duck with buckwheat and mushrooms

To add to the charm of the dining scene, many of the city's Gothic cellars have been converted into romantic restaurants, with brick walls and round arches lending a rustic feel to interiors. In summer, restaurants and cafés put tables outside, along lively streets or in romantic courtyards. When it comes to drinks, Polish beer is renowned. Two great brews are *Żywiec* and *Okocim*. And you must try the famous Kraków vodka at least once!

WHERE KRAKÓW EATS

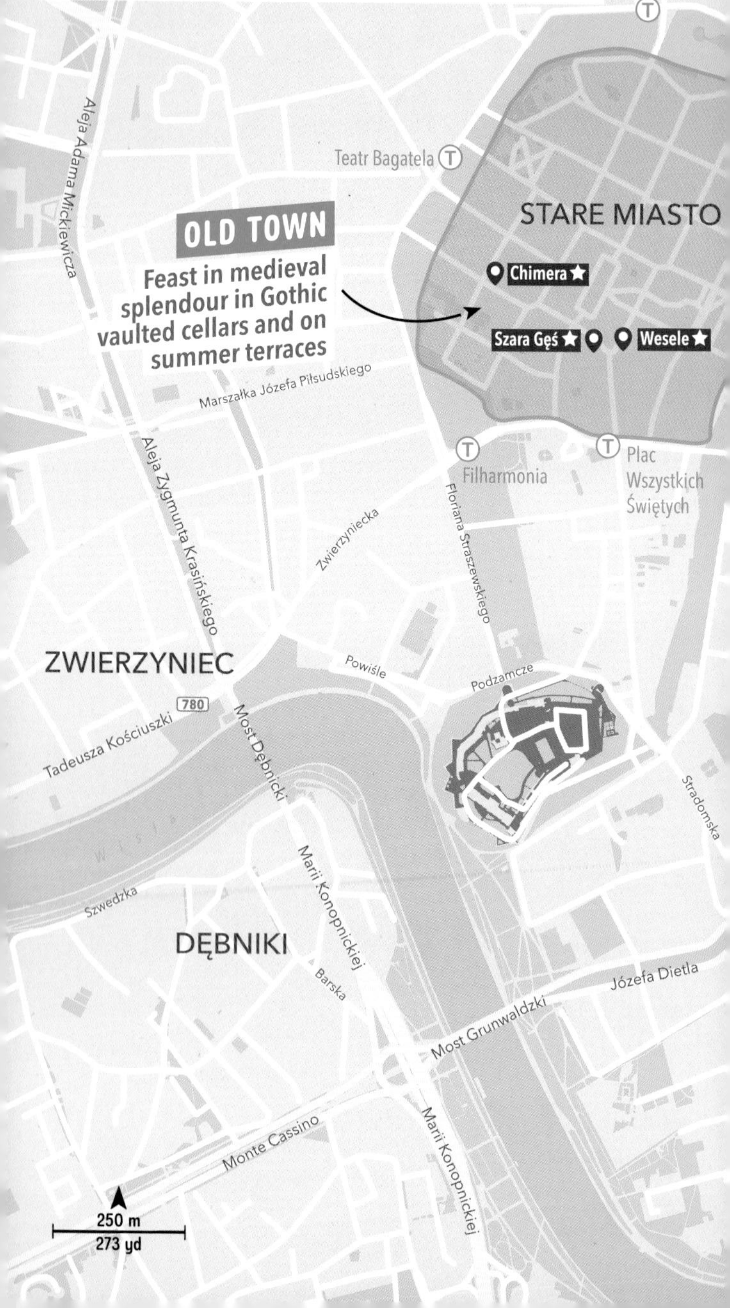

OLD TOWN

Feast in medieval splendour in Gothic vaulted cellars and on summer terraces

Chimera ★
Szara Gęś ★
Wesele ★

STARE MIASTO
ZWIERZYNIEC
DĘBNIKI

Stary Kleparz
Teatr Bagatela
Filharmonia
Plac Wszystkich Świętych
Aleja Adama Mickiewicza
Marszałka Józefa Piłsudskiego
Aleja Zygmunta Krasińskiego
Zwierzyniecka
Floriana Straszewskiego
Powiśle
Podzamcze
Tadeusza Kościuszki
780
Most Dębnicki
Wisła
Stradomska
Szwedzka
Marii Konopnickiej
Barska
Józefa Dietla
Most Grunwaldzki
Monte Cassino
Marii Konopnickiej

250 m
273 yd

MARCO POLO HIGHLIGHTS

★ **CHIMERA**
Huge selection of fresh salads to enjoy in the charming inner courtyard or in front of the fire. ➤ p. 64

★ **SZARA GĘŚ**
Modern Polish cuisine in one of the most beautiful buildings on Market Square. ➤ p. 67

★ **WESELE**
Polish cooking with international flair. ➤ p. 67

★ **ORZO**
Healthy food in a green, jungle-like setting. ➤ p. 68

Today, fine Polish cooking focuses on fish (trout and carp) and game. Kraków's traditional dishes include *pierogi* (filled dumplings) and *gołąbki* (cabbage rolls). Crayfish soup, venison and duck are also classics. Soups like *barszcz* (made of beetroot), *żurek* (based on cereal such as flour or oatmeal) and *zupa borowikowa* (boletus mushroom soup) are also popular Polish dishes that are served in almost all restaurants. It's still true that Poles eat a lot of meat, but pork, veal, poultry and lamb (sometimes served with traditional groats) are no longer the only options. Vegetarian Polish food and even vegan fare are increasingly popular on Kraków's culinary scene. Even *pierogi*, the national dish, is sometimes made without meat; meatless versions have been popular for quite some time.

Kraków's history has had a massive influence on today's diverse, international culinary scene. The Jews introduced kosher and sweet-and-sour dishes. During the Habsburg period, immigrants made Czech, Hungarian and Austrian food popular and they brought their coffee culture with them. Over time, Spanish, Asian, Mexican, Greek and Indian food also began to be served in the city. And let's not forget Italian cooking, also popular here! Kraków also has many of its own specialities, like *obwarzanek*. This ring-shaped bread is braided, baked to perfection and usually sold on the street. The Polish twist on pizza is called *zapiekanka*. This tasty snack is a toasted open sandwich topped with mushrooms, vegetables or ham.

Most restaurants, including the best and most expensive ones, are in the city centre and Kazimierz. Lunch is served around noon and is Kraków's most important meal of the day. Dinner is usually served between 6pm and 7pm, and almost all restaurants open daily and close late unless otherwise noted. Many bistros start serving breakfast at 8am and most cafés sell snacks, too. Smoking is prohibited in all restaurants.

CAFÉS & CAKE SHOPS

1 JAMA MICHALIKA

Art doesn't pay, right? Wrong … kind of. This café is one of the city's oldest, and the interior still boasts the same art nouveau decoration it had when it opened in 1895. At the start of the 20th century, many students from the art academy paid their bills with artwork, proving that art can be a profitable profession after all. The cakes and small plates are as excellent as ever. *Ulica Floriańska 45 | tel. 1 24 22 15 61 | jamamichalika.pl* | Old Town | d2

2 CAMELOT CAFÉ

The café's collection of naïve paintings by Polish painter Nikifor is one of the largest in the country. The folk art is complemented perfectly by the typically Polish wooden cupboards, glass display cases and hand-painted boxes, just like you'd find in a rustic country parlour. The salads are excellent, the apple pie famous citywide and the spirits homemade. The

INSIDER TIP
Folk art and rustic furnishings

Try the world's most expensive coffee in Pożegnanie z Afryką

outdoor seating area is beautifully snug. *Ulica św. Tomasza 17 | tel. 1 24 21 01 23 | FB: camelotcafekrakow |* *Old Town* | d3

3 KAWIARNIA NOWOROLSKI

A traditional, chic Viennese-style café serving amazing cake. The gâteau made with three different kinds of chocolate is amazing! Grab a table on Market Square and enjoy a view of St Mary's Church. *Rynek Główny 1/3 | tel. 5 15 10 09 98 | noworolski.com.pl* | *Old Town* | c4

4 CAFÉ MANGGHA

Located in the Japanese Museum, with a superb view of Wawel Hill from the terrace. You'll find a wide variety of teas served in traditional Japanese clay pots and small cups, plus Japanese beer, sushi and sour-cherry tart. *Closed Mon | Ulica Marii Konopnickiej 26 | tel. 6 08 67 93 08 | FB* | *Dębniki* | B9–10

INSIDER TIP **Japanese treats**

5 POŻEGNANIE Z AFRYKĄ

You'll feel as if you'd died and gone to coffee heaven! The coffee varieties here are endless. Order a fresh cup of joe or take a bag home with you. The world's most exclusive and expensive coffee is also sold here: Kopi Luwak from Indonesia. Only 300–400kg are produced each year. Check out the small museum with coffee-making equipment from yesteryear. *Ulica św. Tomasza 21 | tel. 1 24 21 23 39| pozegnanie.com* | *Old Town* | d3

6 NAKIELNY & WENTZL

Alas, the famous patisserie on the first floor of Hotel Wentzl is no more. Luckily, its successor still serves coffee and sweet treats, as well as breakfast and savoury options. Plus, the location on Market Square couldn't be much

Essential fuel for exploring the Old Town

better. *Rynek Główny 19 | tel. 7 34 64 64 03 | nakielny.pl | Old Town | c4*

ICE-CREAM PARLOURS

7 LODY SI GELA

Ever tried beer ice-cream? Or gorgonzola ice-cream with nuts? Vegan ice-cream? Ice-cream with no artificial flavours? To experience all these and more, give this place a try. Their homemade flavours include lavender and rose petal. *Ulica Staromostowa 1 | FB | Podgórze | E–F11*

8 PRACOWNIA CUKIERNICZA STANISŁAW SARGA

INSIDER TIP
Perfection in a small space

This mini shop offers only six kinds of ice-cream – but perhaps that's exactly why it's the best in town. Try chocolate ice-cream with great chunks of chocolate and strawberry ice-cream with whole strawberries – fantastic! Be prepared to queue. *Closed Sun | Ulica Starowiślna 83 | tram 13 św. Wawrzyńca | Kazimierz | F9*

SNACKS & INFORMAL DINING

9 CHIMERA ★

Do you prefer fresh vegetables to meat? Then you've come to the right place. The salad bar is 30m long and placed in an area covered by a glass roof. Pick what you like and pay either 24 *zł* for a small salad or 29 *zł* for a large one. Grills and soups are also served. A fire is lit in winter. In the 14th-century cellar, the *Nowa Reforma (nowareforma.pl)* restaurant serves Polish specialities. *Świętej Anny 3 | tel. 1 22 92 12 12 | chimera.com.pl | Old Town | b4*

10 KROWARZYWA

No animals were sacrificed to give the patties at this burger joint their delicious taste! You'll find vegan burgers, wraps, hot dogs and kebabs, all bursting with fresh vegetables. Homemade lemonade and smoothies are also available. *Closed Mon | Ulica Sławkowska 8 | tel. 5 31 77 71 36 | krowarzywa.pl/en | Old Town | c3*

11 PIEROGARNIA KRAKOWIACY

Indulge in delicious *pierogi* with modern twists: duck and apple, sauerkraut, buckwheat and cheese or mushrooms. There are always a few veggie options on the menu, as well as typical Polish

Today's Specials

Starters

BARSZCZ
Beetroot soup served with eggs, potatoes and croquettes (also served as a main course)

ROSOŁ
Meat bouillon with pasta

ZUREK
Sour cereal-based soup with boiled eggs, sausage and potatoes

Snacks

OBWARZANEK
Ring-shaped bread that is braided together

ZAPIEKANKA
Half a baguette served open with mushrooms, vegetables or ham

Main courses

PIEROGI
Large dumplings made with a variety of fillings: boiled potatoes and quark *(ruskie)*, meat *(mięsem)*, sauerkraut and mushrooms *(kapustą i grzybami)*, strawberries *(truskawkami)* or plums *(śliwkami)*

GOŁĄBKI
Cabbage leaves stuffed with a filling of rice and meat; a vegetarian version with rice and mushrooms is also common

POTRAWKA CIELĘCA
Veal stew

BIGOS
Meat, sausage, sauerkraut and mushroom stew; also served with red wine

KACZKA Z JABŁKAMI
Roast duck with apple

Sides

KASZA GRYCZANA
Boiled buckwheat groats

MIZERIA
Sweet and sour cucumber salad with sour cream and dill

ZIEMNIAKI OPIEKANE
Roast potatoes

Desserts

SERNIK
Cheesecake

NALEŚNIKI
Sweet pancakes

soups and cakes. The staff wear traditional costumes and the décor is lovingly authentic. And it's self-service, which means it's nice and cheap. *Ulica Szewska 23 | tel. 1 24 22 21 69 | FB: Pierogarnia Krakowiacy | Old Town | b3*

12 PIEROGI MR VINCENT

A restaurant serving over 30 different kinds of *pierogi* dumplings. There's one called *kreplach*, which is a Jewish speciality. They also have *pelmeni*, a Russian delicacy stuffed with meat. *Ulica Bożego Ciała 12 | tel. 5 06 80 63 04 | tram 1, 10, 12, 22, 52 Stradom | FB: pierogivincent | Kazimierz | E9*

PIZZERIAS

13 PIZZATOPIA

INSIDER TIP
Craft your own pizza

Create your own pizza masterpiece! Choose your favourite toppings and don't be afraid to get creative. Everything is placed on light and fluffy dough and takes less than three minutes to bake. They also have delicious salads, homemade lemonade and bottled craft beer. Dishes are served on wooden platters. *Ulica Szewska 22 | tel. 5 70 06 51 95 | pizzatopia.com | Old Town | b3*

14 TRZY PAPRYCZKI

Transport yourself to Italy in this rustically decorated restaurant serving more than 20 different kinds of pizza, along with a selection of antipasti, pasta and salads. *Ulica Poselska 17 | tel. 5 17 02 23 12 | trzypapryczki.krakow.pl | Old Town | d6*

RESTAURANTS £££

15 FARINA

Fish? In Kraków?! Well, of course! This is one of the best fish and seafood restaurants in the city. They offer seasonal dishes and everything from oysters to gilt headed bream. Excellent meat and pasta dishes are also available. *Ulica św. Marka 16 | tel. 5 19 39 94 74 | farina.com.pl | Old Town | d2*

16 HAWEŁKA – RESTAURACJA TETMAJEROWSKA

This restaurant has been serving exclusive Polish and international cuisine in a *fin-de-siècle* ambience since 1876. The staircase is adorned with paintings by Polish art nouveau artists. There is a wide choice of game and fish dishes. The ground floor is home to a slightly less expensive version of the restaurant. The *Hawełka Cake Shop* in the entrance passageway offers sweet things to take away. *Rynek Główny 34 | tel. 1 24 22 06 31 | FB | Old Town | c3*

17 PIMIENTO

With two locations, this restaurant is all about meat – and a little bit of seafood – often tucked away in fabulous ravioli. The steaks, some of which are truly enormous and include Wagyu and Kobe beef, really do taste as good as they look. There's a good choice of wines from all over the globe. Booking recommended in the evening. *Ulica Stolarska 13 | tel. 1 24 22 66 72 | Old Town | d5. Ulica Józefa 26 | tel. 1 24 21 25 02 | Kazimierz | E9 | pimiento.pl*

18 SZARA

Restaurant with a charming setting in a medieval townhouse with Gothic arches. Exquisite European dishes: *raraka* (potato fritters with caviar), reindeer or salmon tartare. A less expensive lunch is served from noon to 3pm, which you can eat outside in summer while enjoying the view of St Mary's Church. The bar has excellent cocktails. *Rynek Główny 6 | tel. 1 24 21 66 69 | szara.pl | Old Town | d4*

19 SZARA GĘŚ ★

You may struggle to concentrate on the food here at the "Grey Goose" because your surroundings – a 13th-century house with Gothic vaults – are so magnificent. The restaurant serves modern Polish cuisine with regional ingredients in the most enchanting ambience. Choose from à la carte or a five- or seven-course menu tasting menu *(360 zł/460 zł)*. The only downside: the interior is so beautiful that you won't want to sit outside in summer! *Rynek Główny 17 | tel. 1 24 30 63 11 | szarages.com | Old Town | c4*

20 WESELE ★

With a view of the Market Square, this restaurant on two floors serves modern Polish cooking and Kraków specialities. Try delicious combination platters like Polish potato pancakes with sour cream or duck with honey-dipped pears. *Rynek Główny 10 | tel.*

Follow the signs to Restaurant Szara

1 24 22 74 60 | weselerestauracja.pl | Old Town | 🕮 c4

21 WIERZYNEK

Over 650 years ago, the monarchs of Europe had a feast here lasting 20 days and nights. Today, it's the city's most famous restaurant. Your feast won't last as long, of course, but you'll be treated to a royal experience nonetheless. Overlooking the Market Square, the rooms are all beautifully decorated, and delicious Polish and international specialities are served. Evening meals are by reservation only. *Rynek Główny 16 | tel. 7 28 87 10 71 | wierzynek.pl/en | Old Town | 🕮 c4*

RESTAURANTS ££

22 ORZO ★

The food made here follows the motto "people, music, nature". The menu offers burgers, pizza, salad – and the eponymous rice-shaped pasta called orzo. Healthy ingredients are added, and the tastes blend wonderfully with the restaurant's jungle-like atmosphere. Escape the notorious city smog and breathe in the clear air created by the hanging plants, small shrubs and trees. *Lipowa 4a | tel. 1 28 89 99 72 | orzo.pl | Zabłocie | 🕮 H10*

23 ZAKŁADKA FOOD & WINE

Oh là là! An original French bistro in a stunning 18th-century building. The menu includes local products such as goats' cheese and freshly caught trout from Ojców National Park. Ensure you make a reservation if it's the weekend! *Ulica Józefińska 2 | tel. 1 24 42 74 42 | zakladkabistro.pl | trams 3, 6, 8–11, 13, 17, 19, 20, 24, 50 Korona | Podgórze | 🕮 F11*

24 DINE IN THE DARK

The "dining in the dark" theme has reached Kraków, but the experience here comes with a twist. We don't want to spoil it, but it involves Polish (vegetarian) cuisine. Book early online to avoid disappointment as the experience has become very popular. *At restaurant Piwnica pod Kominkiem: Ulica Bracka 13 | tel. 1 24 30 21 30 | dineinthedark.pl | Old Town | 🕮 c5*

25 KLEZMER-HOIS ⚑

Jewish food, but not kosher, and an authentic atmosphere, with lace tablecloths, old, dark furniture and paintings commonly seen in bourgeois homes of the mid 20th century. The unforgettable dining experience that takes you into another world, especially when one of the klezmer concerts is taking place (usually at the weekend). *Ulica Szeroka 6 | tel. 1 24 11 12 45 | klezmer.pl | tram 24 Ulica Miodowa | Kazimierz | 🕮 F9*

26 POD ANIOŁAMI

The finest Polish cuisine served in a Gothic cellar. Grilled meat, pies (such as hare pie with cranberries) and duck with apples are served with dark wholemeal bread, red cabbage and sour pickles. In summer, guests are served in a small courtyard outside in the garden. Good wine list and Polish mead. *Ulica Grodzka 35 | tel. 1 24 30 21 13 | podaniolami.pl | Old Town | 🕮 c6*

Healthy ingredients and a stylish setting are the winning combination at Orzo

27 RESTAURACJA TRADYCJA

Does Polish folk dancing increase one's appetite? There's only one way to find out! Every Saturday at 7pm, guests are invited to a folklore dining and dancing experience, with opportunities to participate. If you'd like something unique, try the Polish-Italian main course. The restaurant is on Market Square in a Renaissance building where Hieronim Pinocci lived in the 16th century. He was the Italian king's secretary and published Poland's first newspaper. *Rynek Główny 15 | tel. 1 24 24 96 16 | tradycyja.pl | Old Town | c4–5*

RESTAURANTS £

28 DOBRA KASZA NASZA

SIDER TIP
Groats galore!

Groats anyone? These ground cereal grains are made of buckwheat, millet or pearl barley and are a staple of Polish cuisine. This restaurant serves them covered with a meat- or vegetable-based sauce. *Rynek Główny 28 | tel. 5 31 62 64 47 | dobrakaszanasza.pl | Old Town | b4*

29 KOLANKO NUMER 6

This place offers a great breakfast buffet, international cuisine and all kinds of sweet and savoury crêpes. Guests are served on the beautiful green terrace in summer *Ulica Józefa 17 | tel. 5 09 66 99 59 | kolanko.net | tram 8 Plac Wolnica | Kazimierz | E9*

30 POLAKOWSKI

A self-service restaurant serving good homemade Polish dishes, soups and meat at great prices. *Ulica Miodowa 39 | polakowski.com.pl | Kazimierz | E9*

SHOPPING

You can find all the international brands and chains in Kraków, but there's a lot more here, with a good sprinkling of independent shops selling locally made goods that make great souvenirs. Shopping in the city centre is particularly enjoyable as many stores are located in historic buildings.

Shops line Market Square, the Royal Route, Ulica Floriańska and Ulica Grodzka. Here, you'll find everything from delicatessens to fashion boutiques, along with art and bric-a-brac. In Kazimierz, you'll find charming modern art galleries, designer jeweller and a popular

You'll find all the venues in this chapter on the pull-out mape

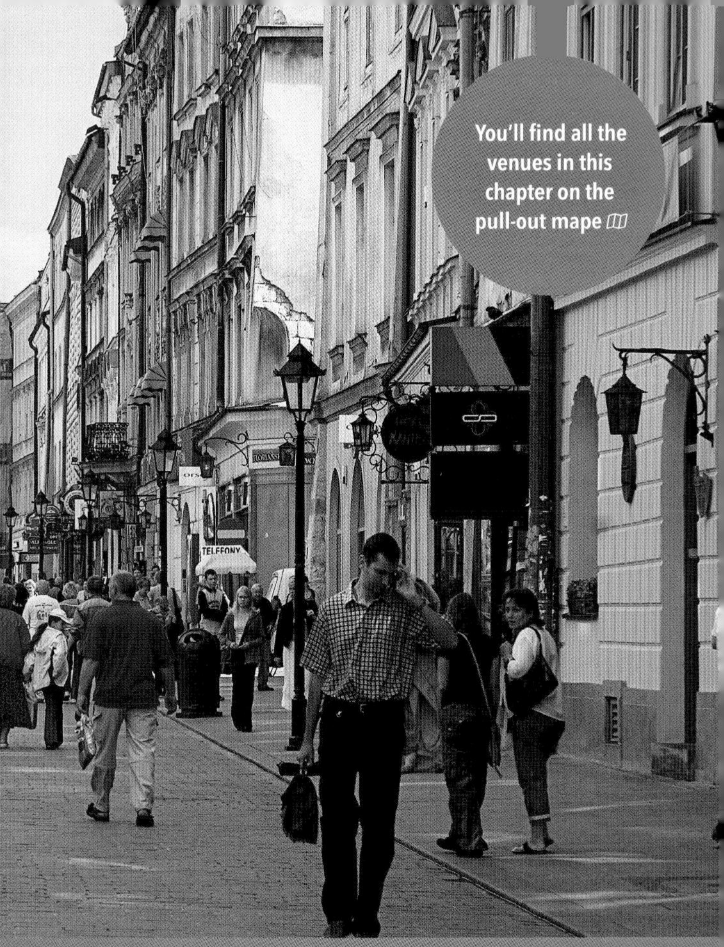

Ulica Florianska offers modern shopping in a historical atmosphere

Sunday flea market. If you're in the market to buy something unique to take home, visit one of the city's amber jewellery shops. Poland is known for its high-quality spirits, including *Żubrówka* (bison grass vodka), *Krupnik* (honey liqueur) and *Żołądkowa Gorzka* (herbal vodka). If you need something for the kids, they'll love a Wawel Dragon or one of the traditional wooden toys you'll find for sale.

For general information on opening hours, see the Good to Know section (p. 116). Where they deviate significantly from the norm, we have listed them here.

WHERE KRAKÓW SHOPS

AROUND RYNEK GŁÓWNY

Find holiday souvenirs in abundance here

ULICA JÓZEFA

Looking for somethi
unusual or specia
Kazimierz is the perf
place to brow

Stary Kleparz
KROWODRZA
STARE MIASTO
Teatr Bagatela
Wedel
Bukowski
Filharmonia
Plac Wszystkich Świętych
Ambra Stile
Zwierzyniecka
Floriana Straszewskiego
Aleja Adama Mickiewicza
ZWIERZYNIEC
Powiśle
Podzamcze
780
Most Dębnicki
Stradomska
MariiKonopnickiej
DĘBNIKI
Barska
Most Grunwaldzki
200 m
219 yd

ULICA FLORIAŃSKA & ULICA GRODZKA

Time for some high-end shopping? Fashion, art and antiques line these two boulevards

MARCO POLO HIGHLIGHTS

★ **BUKOWSKI**
Adorable teddy bears and dolls for children of all ages. The fluffy alphabet letters are charming. ➤ p. 75

★ **PLAC TARGOWY UNITARG**
Rummage until the cows come home: every Sunday, the usual food market turns into a wild flea market. ➤ p. 76

★ **AMBRA STILE**
Remarkable amber jewellery, and pieces made with other materials, too. Worth browsing for that special item! ➤ p. 76

★ **WEDEL**
Handmade chocolates, drinking chocolate and mouth-watering desserts – a treat for over 150 years. ➤ p. 77

BOOKS

1 DE REVOLUTIONIBUS

Reading Copernicus's *De revolutionibus et orbium celestium (On the Revolutions of the Celestial Spheres)* in the original will certainly improve your Latin, and you can enjoy it with coffee, cake or a smoothie here. You'll find plenty of Polish- and English-language books, including Copernicus's literary masterpiece. *Rynek Podgórski 8 | derevolutionibus.pl | Podgórze | F12*

2 EMPIK

This branch of the Kraków music and bookstore chain is housed in a building that has sold books since 1610, making it the first bookstore in Europe. The interior has been completely renovated, revealing old portals, impressive ceilings and a beautiful area now occupied by a café. *Rynek Główny 23 | Old Town | c4*

INSIDER TIP
Europe's oldest bookstore

WHERE TO START?

In addition to **Galeria Krakowska** and **Galeria Kazimierz**, the most popular places to go shopping are **Ulica Floriańska** and **Ulica Grodzka**. This is where you will find fashion, shoe stores and jewellery shops, not to mention a number of art galleries and antique dealers. There are also many souvenir shops in and around **Rynek Główny**, the Market Square, and **Cloth Hall**. If you're looking for original styles, you'll find plenty of unique jewellery and out-of-the-ordinary souvenirs on **Ulica Józefa** in Kazimierz (take tram 6 or 8 to Plac Wolnica).

SHOPPING CENTRES

3 GALERIA KAZIMIERZ

This is Kraków's most impressive shopping centre. The building has an original design and a brick exterior. Inside, you'll find over 100 shops, cafés, restaurants and even a cinema. *Ulica Podgórska 34 | galeriakazimierz.pl | trams 3, 9, 19, 24 to św. Wawrzynca, then a 5-min walk along the Vistula | Kazimierz | G9*

4 GALERIA KRAKOWSKA

A shopping centre with over 270 shops covering a floor space of 36,000m². You'll find brand-name sports, fashion and cosmetic goods for sale, as well as cafés and restaurants. *Ulica Pawia 5 | galeriakrakowska.pl | Kleparz | f1*

5 PASAŻ HANDLOWY 13

If "Gothic", "Renaissance", "metal" and "glass" float your boat, well just seeing this exclusive department store on Market Square will make your trip! In addition to many Polish fashion labels, you'll also find exclusive delicacies from around the world. They offer a large selection of Italian wines, which you can savour at the bar or in the underground restaurant. *Rynek Główny 13 | pasaz-13.pl | Old Town | c5*

CHILDREN

6 BAJO

A cult address for eco-friendly wooden toys. The products range from tiny figures and cars to wooden horses and doll's prams. The Gruffalo toys are particularly amusing. *Ulica Grodzka 60 | bajo.eu | Old Town | D8*

7 CIUCIU CUKIER ARTIST

This confectioner offers workshop tours, during which young confectioners in training can learn how the sweet treats are made and then make their own candy creations! If this doesn't give you enough of a sugar shock, head over to the shop to buy some handmade goodies to take home with you. The sweets follow recipes from the 17th and 18th centuries! *Workshop tours start at 11am and repeat every hour | children 10 zł, carers free | Ulica Grodzka 38 | ciuciukrakow.pl/en | Old Town | c6*

SIDER TIP
Make your own sweets

8 BUKOWSKI ★

A dream for teddy bear lovers! Four hundred of the stuffed toys fill wooden shelves from floor to ceiling. They come in all sizes. *Ulica Sienna 1 | galeriabukowski.pl | Old Town | d4*

ART GALLERIES

9 GALERIA GOŁOGÓRSKI

Run by artist Marian Gołogórski, this gallery specialises in modern Polish painting and sculpture made of metal, stone and glass. *Tue–Fri 4–8pm, Sat 11am–3pm | Ulica Grodzka 29 | gologorski.com | Old Town | c6*

Teddy bears at Bukowski

10 JAN FEJKIEL GALLERY

This gallery has the largest stock of modern Polish graphic art and drawings in the city. It places great importance on supporting young Kraków artists and organises many exhibitions. *Mon–Fri 11am–6pm, Sat 11am–3pm | Ulica Sławkowska 14 | fejkielgallery.com | Old Town | c2*

MARKETS

11 NOWY KLEPARZ

The people of Kraków have been shopping here since 1925. Flowers, fruit, vegetables, cosmetics and everything else you could ever want. *Ulica Długa/ corner of Aleja Słowackiego | kleparz.krakow.pl | Kleparz | C2*

Sweets galore at Wedel

12 PLAC TARGOWY UNITARG ★

A flea market is held here every Sunday (there's a food market during the week). You will find all kinds of goods – from old radios to Meissen porcelain – and at fair prices too. *Ulica Grzegórzecka | unitarg.krakow.pl | tram 1 Hala Targowa | Grzegórzki | F7*

FASHION & ACCESSORIES

13 CLICK FASHION

With two locations, this store offers a tasteful selection of women's fashion that's made right here in Kraków. You'll find many designs, ranging from quietly modest to extraordinary. *Ulica Grodzka 32 | Old Town | c6. Ulica Krakowska 14 | Kazimierz | D–E 9–10 | clickfashion.pl*

14 MIĘTA DESIGN

The shop and showroom of a young Kraków designer. Choose from bright and distinctive small bags, or opt for a rucksack, purse or suitcase. And there are often deals on prices, too. *Ulica Szlak 32/1 | mieta.eu | Kleparz | D3*

15 WITTCHEN

Exclusive products made in Poland. Leather bags, cases, gloves, jackets, umbrellas and exquisite luggage. *Ulica Podgórska 34 | Galeria Kazimierz | wittchen.com | Kazimierz | G9*

16 FORUM MODY

More than 60 Polish designers have taken over the rooms of the former Hotel Cracovia, where they sell the latest in fashion and accessories. Take a look at sister offering *Forum Designu (forumdesignu.pl):* their furniture, home accessories and art are varied, exciting and on trend. *Ulica Focha 1 | forumdesignu.pl/22-forum-mody | Półwsie Zwierzyniecki | A7*

JEWELLERY

17 AMBRA STILE ★

Predominantly Italian silver jewellery with semi-precious stones and pearls, as well as pieces with amber and wonderfully unique locally made items – from cufflinks to small ants and lizards with amber bodies. *Plac Dominikański 2 | ambrastile.krakow.pl | Old Town | c5*

18 BLAZKO JEWELLERY

Here you'll find attractive silver jewellery with a black-and-white finish – a style that is the hallmark of Grzegorz Błażko's store. Brightly coloured pieces are available too. *Ulica Józefa 11 | blazko.pl | Kazimierz | E9*

19 AMBER JEWELLERY

An array of jewellery, spoons, chess games and cufflinks. The products offered are made from real natural amber and come with a certificate of authenticity. The jewellery made from striped flint from Sandomierz makes very special and unusual souvenirs. *Plac Mariacki 9 | s-a.pl | Old Town | d4*

INSIDER TIP
Flint jewellery to take home

SOUVENIRS

20 BROKAT

Here you'll find exquisite fabric items such as dolls, handmade cushions and tea cosies. Many of pieces are made by the students of Kraków's art academy. *Ulica Bracka 9 | Old Town | c5*

21 ĆMIELÓW PORCELANA

The largest producer of fine porcelain in Europe. The store offers lovely sets of china and, for collectors, a small series of porcelain figures. *Ulica Stradomska 3 | porcelana.pl | Stradom | Ds8*

22 GALERIA

Galeria has many souvenirs created by Kraków-based artists, using glass, ceramics, clay and wood. The hand-painted furniture is especially attractive, but probably too large to fit in your suitcase! *Ulica Grodzka 60 | Old Town | D8*

INSIDER TIP
Artistic souvenirs

23 REGIONALNE ALKOHOLE

This beautiful liquor store offers shelf after shelf of regional beer, wines, spirits and vodka. *Ulica Miodowa 28a | regionalnealkohole.com | Kazimierz | E9*

24 SUKIENNICE (CLOTH HALL) ★

On Market Square, you'll find the largest selection of Kraków-made souvenirs, ranging from jewellery and wooden articles to leather bags, traditional clothing, ceramics and glass articles. *Rynek Główny 2 | Old Town | c4*

SWEETS

25 WEDEL ★

Traditional confectioners selling handmade pralines, chocolates and sweets. Two of their delicious specialities are *torcik wedlowski* (a chocolate-covered wafer with layers of chocolate-and-nut cream) and *ptasie mleczko* (milk chocolate truffles filled with cream). You can sample the delicacies in the café next door. *Rynek Główny 46 | wedel pijalnie.pl | Old Town | d3*

NIGHTLIFE

Few cities in the world have nightlife as young, colourful and exciting as Kraków's. The best thing about this city is its unique character – people here refuse to follow every international trend, and that goes for after-dark entertainment too. The city's nightlife has its own, very distinctive distinctive ambience.

Kazimierz is dominated by everything quirky, alternative and artsy, attracting students and artists. You can party until dawn in the district's dimly lit cafés, clubs and pubs. Along and around Plac Nowy, several old, partially renovated buildings and cellars have been

Night owls flock to Plac Nowy in Kazimierz

converted. Inside, you'll often find mismatched tables, antique sofas, cinema chairs and school desks, plus exhibitions by young artists, and modern theatre and cabaret shows. The vibe around Kazimierz is always buzzing, guaranteeing a night full of fun and artistic encounters. Podgórze's nightlife is also blossoming. On beautiful summer nights, the river beckons and the boulevards around the Vistula come alive.

WHERE KRAKÓW GOES OUT

Batorego
Stary Kleparz
KROWODRZA
Park im.
H. Jordana
Aleja Adama Mickiewicza
Teatr Bagatela
Piano Rouge ★
Harris Piano Jazz Bar ★
STARE MIASTO
Uniwersytet
Jagielloński
Krakowskie Błonia
Filharmonia Krakowska
(Kraków Philharmonic) ★
Aleja Marszałka Ferdynanda Focha
Stadion
Cracovii
Filharmonia
Plac
Wszystkich
Świętych
Zwierzyniecka
ZWIERZYNIEC
Powiśle
Podzamcze
Księcia Józefa
780
Szwedzka
Marii Konopnickiej
Józefa Dietla
Monte Cassino

MARCO POLO HIGHLIGHTS

★ **HARRIS PIANO JAZZ BAR**
Trad jazz, jam sessions, blues nights and international stars – all kinds of jazz at one of the city's most famous live music clubs. ➤ p. 85

★ **PIANO ROUGE**
It's not only the interior that's luxurious; the music and Indian cuisine are also top class. ➤ p. 85

★ **ALCHEMIA**
Location with a cult following, at the epicentre of Kasimierz's pulsating nightlife scene. ➤ p. 85

★ **FILHARMONIA KRAKOWSKA (KRAKÓW PHILHARMONIC)**
Symphonies performed by one of the best orchestras in the country, as well as organ recitals and jazz concerts. ➤ p. 87

PODGÓRZE

The nightlife zone along the Vistula is picking up momentum

Rakowicka
Aleksandra Lubomirskiego
Kraków Główny
Mogilska
Lubicz
Aleja Powstania Warszawskiego
RYNEK GŁÓWNY
Sharp dresses and high heels are the order of the day in upscale clubs and stylish jazz venues
Ogród Botaniczny Uniwersytetu Jagiellońskiego
Aleja Pokoju
Grzegórzecka
KAZIMIERZ
GRZEGÓRZKI
Starowiślna
Klezmer music, an arty crowd and students come together to create an uproariously fun pub and bar scene
Nowy Cmentarz Żydowski
Miodowa
Alchemia
Wisła
Św. Wawrzyńca
Zabłocie
Muzeum Inżynierii Miejskiej
Dajwór
Podgórska
Stanisława Klimeckiego
Plac Bohaterów Getta
Kalwaryjska
Bolesława Limanowskiego
776
Korona
Powstańców Wielkopolskich
Park Bednarskiego
PODGÓRZE
Aleja Powstańców Śląskich
Wielicka
776
400 m
437 yd

The nightlife in the city centre is often tamer than in the surrounding districts, and caters more often for tourists. In the Old Town, it is more likely that you will be asked for ID or be turned away by a bouncer for not being properly dressed. Most clubs and pubs are located in and around Rynek Główny and are best reached on foot. Most pubs are underground in beautifully renovated cellars, and many have an inner courtyard or garden.

And then there's jazz – the music for which the city is best known. Many jazz musicians live here for this reason, including the exceptional violinist Nigel Kennedy, who plays jazz as well as classical music. In addition to his regular concerts at the Kraków Philharmonic, he often performs in jazz clubs (and klezmer concerts), as well. Many pubs and clubs also function as music venues/restaurants/dance clubs. In Kraków, they don't see a reason to separate these functions and love blurring the lines.

Kraków also has its fair share of high culture, with the Kraków Philharmonic Hall and the Opera House for classical performances, as well as many theatres. Some events are even held outdoors or in unusual locations, such as the arcaded courtyard of the Royal Castle or one of Kraków's many churches. Keep in mind that the churches are usually not heated, so be sure to bring a light pullover, even in summer.

Women don't usually have to pay an admission fee at the clubs. Men, however, are required to pay 20–30 *zł* to get in. In most cases, everyone gets into the clubs for free after 1am or so. Some clubs demand guests be 21 to enter, and there are strict rules to follow at all locations. If you're under 18, you're not allowed alcohol and cigarettes. When you go out, only take the valuables and cash you need as the clubs tend to be packed at weekends and thefts can happen.

INSIDER TIP
Travel light

Kraków also has lovely little cinemas showing films in their original language, with Polish subtitles.

WHERE TO START?

Kraków's coolest jazz venues are below ground in medieval cellars, while the best clubs and pubs line the streets around **Rynek Główny**, most of them in the pedestrianised area. Klezmer music is performed in many of the Jewish restaurants on **Ulica Szeroka** in **Kazimierz**. If you're looking for a night out on the town, **Plac Nowy** is the place to be for those wanting to party in the pubs or celebrate outdoors on the streets. Tram no. 24 (Ulica Miodowa) takes you directly into the heart of Kazimierz's nightlife zone.

NIGHTCLUBS

1 FORUM PRZESTRZENIE

This bistro/music club is a great spot to get the night rolling and a popular hangout for artists. The food is also good. Chill out on a lounger outside

It's not just jazz on the sound system in Kraków's clubs

and relax by the Vistula. Open-air concerts and exhibitions take place frequently. *Daily 10am–4am | Ulica Marii Konopnickiej 28 | mob. 5 14 34 29 39 | forumprzestrzenie.com | Ludwinów | ▯ C11*

2 B4

House, R'n'B and old school threaten to draw you onto one of several dancefloors at this laid-back music club. If that isn't enough of a temptation, there's also a café, gallery, plenty of live concerts and special deals via Facebook. *Daily | Ulica Bracka 4 | FB: bracka4 | Old Town | ▯ c4–5*

3 JAZZ ROCK CAFE

Don't let "jazz" in the name give you the wrong impression. This is actually a cult address for rock music, so get ready to rock out! Two rooms, two bars and a proper loud sound. Perfect for those wanting to lose themselves in the music or see a live show. *Tue–Fri 8pm–5am | Sławkowska 12 | FB | Old Town | ▯ c2*

4 POD JASZCZURAMI

Established in 1960, this is one of the city's oldest student clubs. Its name translates as "Among Lizards". The building dates from medieval times and features a coat of arms above the entrance depicting two little green reptiles (hence the name). It's a café by day and a club by night (from 8pm). There are concerts on Fridays, DJs on Saturdays, and karaoke on Thursdays and Sundays. *Daily from 9am | Rynek Główny 8 | podjaszczurami.pl | Old Town | ▯ c4*

5 PROZAK 2.0

A nightclub in a traditional Kraków cellar, with three dancefloors, four bars and red-and-blue neon lights. Very popular among young people

Relax and soak up the jazz at Piano Rouge

who like dancing to music spun by exceptionally good DJs: funk, disco, electro and house. *Daily from 11pm | Plac Dominkański 6 | FB: Prozak DwaZero | Old Town | c5*

6 LET'S SING KARAOKE BAR

Have you secretly harboured a long-held dream of pop (or rock) stardom? This karaoke bar with a friendly team and laid-back punters is the perfect place to unleash your inner Freddie Mercury or Billie Eilish. *Daily from 8pm | Ulica Grodzka 34 | FB: karaoke barkrakow | Old Town | c6*

7 CHOICE CLUB

Seriously exclusive club with exquisite designer furnishings, a smoking area, two dancefloors and four bars – all serving excellent cocktails to a more discerning crowd (21 and over). The bouncers are strict, so dress up! *Sat 10pm–4am | Ulica Floriańska 15 | choiceclub.pl | Old Town | d3*

8 SHINE CLUB

Finally, a club suitable for that little black dress! This is one of the city's most famous nightclubs, with three bars and dancefloors spread out over 1,000m² of space. It used to be a cinema, but you would never guess thanks to the royally furnished interior, impressively illuminated with LED lighting. Top DJs perform here, playing house music, chart hits, hip-hop and R'n'B. *Fri/Sat 10pm–5pm | Ulica Starowislna 16 | shineclub.com.pl | Wesoła Zachód | f6*

JAZZ

9 HARRIS PIANO JAZZ BAR ★

One of the most famous jazz clubs in Kraków! Several concerts take place here every week *(from 9pm)*: traditional jazz on Tuesday; a jam session on Thursday; blues night on Friday; and international jazz stars on Saturday *(Thu–Sat admission from 30 zł, otherwise free entry)*. Good drinks and an excellent selection of beer are served at one of the longest bars in town. Pizza is available if you're hungry. *Sat/Sun from 10am, otherwise from 11am | Rynek Główny 28 | harris.krakow.pl | Old Town | b4*

10 U MUNIAKA

A jazz club founded by saxophonist Janusz Muniak. Located in a brick-lined cellar with arched ceilings, the club attracts a good mix of artists and musicians, and the atmosphere is superb. Live concerts take place from 9.30pm on several days during the week (see website). *Daily from 7pm | Ulica Florianska 3 | jazzumuniaka.club | Old Town | d3*

11 PIANO ROUGE ★

Red carpets, a chandelier and comfortable sofas make for a plush setting. It's an ideal environment for great jazz concerts *(daily from 8pm or 9pm)*. Burgers and a number of Italian/Polish specialities are also available. *Daily from 10.30am | Rynek Główny 46 | thepianorouge.com | Old Town | d3*

12 PIEC ART

No, you aren't seeing things. The bar here has actually been built inside a massive, partly tiled oven. The bar's name, *piec*, means "oven" in Polish. Guests sit in a beautifully renovated Gothic cellar, and a wide range of cocktails and other drinks are available. On Wednesdays and Thursdays from 8.30pm, live jazz acts alternate between Polish musicians and international stars, and guests are wined and dined at their tables during the show. Fish soup is a speciality. Aged 21 and up only. *Daily from 4pm | Ulica Szewska 21 | piecart.pl | Old Town | b3*

INSIDER TIP
Dinner and jazz

CINEMAS

13 POD BARANAMI

Three air-conditioned auditoriums in a former palace on Market Square. The cinema organises programmes on special themes several times each year; the main focus is on European cinema. There's a small café on the first floor. Films are screened in their original language. *Rynek Główny 27 | Pałac Pod Baranami | kinopodbaranami.pl | Old Town | b4*

PUBS & BARS

14 ALCHEMIA ★

Cult venue in Kazimierz: a stuffed crocodile hangs over the bar and guests can enter a hidden room through a cupboard. Inside the candlelit bar, with un-plastered walls, guests sit on rickety chairs at old tables. The drinks are great, and the apple pie is sensational. Concerts and modern theatre events take place in the cellar. The venue is in the heart of Kazimierz and it's a great spot to sit outside in summer – enjoy watching the young people bar hop between the pubs on Plac Nowy. *Daily from 10am | Ulica Estery 5 | alchemia.com.pl | Kazimierz | E9*

15 OMERTA PUB & MORE

A poster above this bar reads: "Join the Corleone Family." Even if you choose not to become a member of the Mafia clan, you're still welcome to try beers from all over the world. They serve over 30 on tap and 150 bottled craft beers. Evenings are packed, so call to make a reservation. *Daily from 4pm | Ulica Warszauera 3, entrance on Ulica Kupa 3 | tel. 5 01 50 82 27 | FB | Kazimierz | E9*

INSIDER TIP
Beers in a Mafia-themed bar

16 PUB PROPAGANDA

The place to go if you want to feel the communist atmosphere of days gone by: Lenin stares down from a portrait on the walls, which are decorated with old propaganda posters and retro items like record players. You absolutely must try the speciality *wściekły pies* (mad dog) cocktail: the ice-cold vodka with tabasco and raspberry juice really is something special. *Daily from 6pm | pubpropaganda.eu | Ulica Miodowa 20 | Kazimierz | E9*

INSIDER TIP
Mad dog cocktail

17 PUB POD ZIEMIĄ

Enjoy rock, metal and alternative music in this small cellar pub in Kazimierz. Plenty of delicious food and drinks are on offer too. Concerts take place at the weekend and are followed by a night of karaoke. Ladies are treated to cheaper prices on Wednesday. *Daily from 6pm | Ulica Miodowa 43 | pubpodziemia.pl | Kazimierz | E–F9*

18 LE SCANDALE

Why not spend the whole day here? Come for breakfast and stay for burgers, steaks, pizza and drinks. You'll need the energy when night falls and the DJ's music keeps everything in motion. The pub has a beautiful inner courtyard. *Daily from 9am | Plac Nowy 9 | FB: LeScandale Garden | Kazimierz | E9*

19 SINGER

Old Singer sewing machines have been turned into tables at this, the oldest pub in Kazimierz. In summer you can also sit outside in the fresh air. There's a fine selection of alcoholic drinks, as well as coffee and cake. *Daily from 10am | corner of Ulica Izaaka/Estery | Kazimierz | E9*

20 WARSZTAT

A mixture of café and pub. The biggest impression is made by the interior, which is packed with old musical instruments – a piano has even been inserted upright into the bar! This is where the way-out in-crowd meets in Kazimierz. There is music in the background: blues, jazz or klezmer, and

Alchemia is the perfect place to spend those long Kraków winter evenings

beer is served in enormous jugs. *Daily from 9am | Ulica Izaaka 3 | restauracja warsztat.pl | Kazimierz | E9*

OPERA & CLASSICAL MUSIC

21 FILHARMONIA KRAKOWSKA (KRAKÓW PHILHARMONIC) ★

The Kraków Philharmonic Society was founded in 1909 and its orchestra has been housed in this neo-Baroque building since 1930. The Kraków Philharmonic Orchestra and the Radio Symphony Orchestra are two of the best in Poland. Symphony and organ concerts are held in this hall, as are jazz performances and other concerts as part of various festivals (for example, the *Warsaw Beethoven Festival* at Easter). Programme in English.

The Philharmonic also organises *Wawel Evenings (Wieczory wawelskie)*, where chamber music is played in the fabulously atmospheric setting of the castle or in its arcaded courtyard. *Ticket office: Tue 2–7pm, Wed 10am–2pm, Fri 3–9pm and 1 hr before performance | Ulica Zwierzyniecka 1 | filharmonia.krakow.pl | Old Town | a5*

22 OPERA SKA

The multicoloured, segmented complex which houses the Kraków Opera House is the setting for traditional and modern productions of Polish and international operas. The summer festival is very popular, with performances held in the arcaded courtyard of Wawel Castle as well as in the Opera House itself. You'll need to book tickets well in advance! *Ticket office: Mon–Fri 11am–6pm and 2 hrs before performance | tickets 50–100 zł | Ulica Lubicz 48 | opera.krakow.pl | Grzegórzki | G5*

ACTIVE & RELAXED

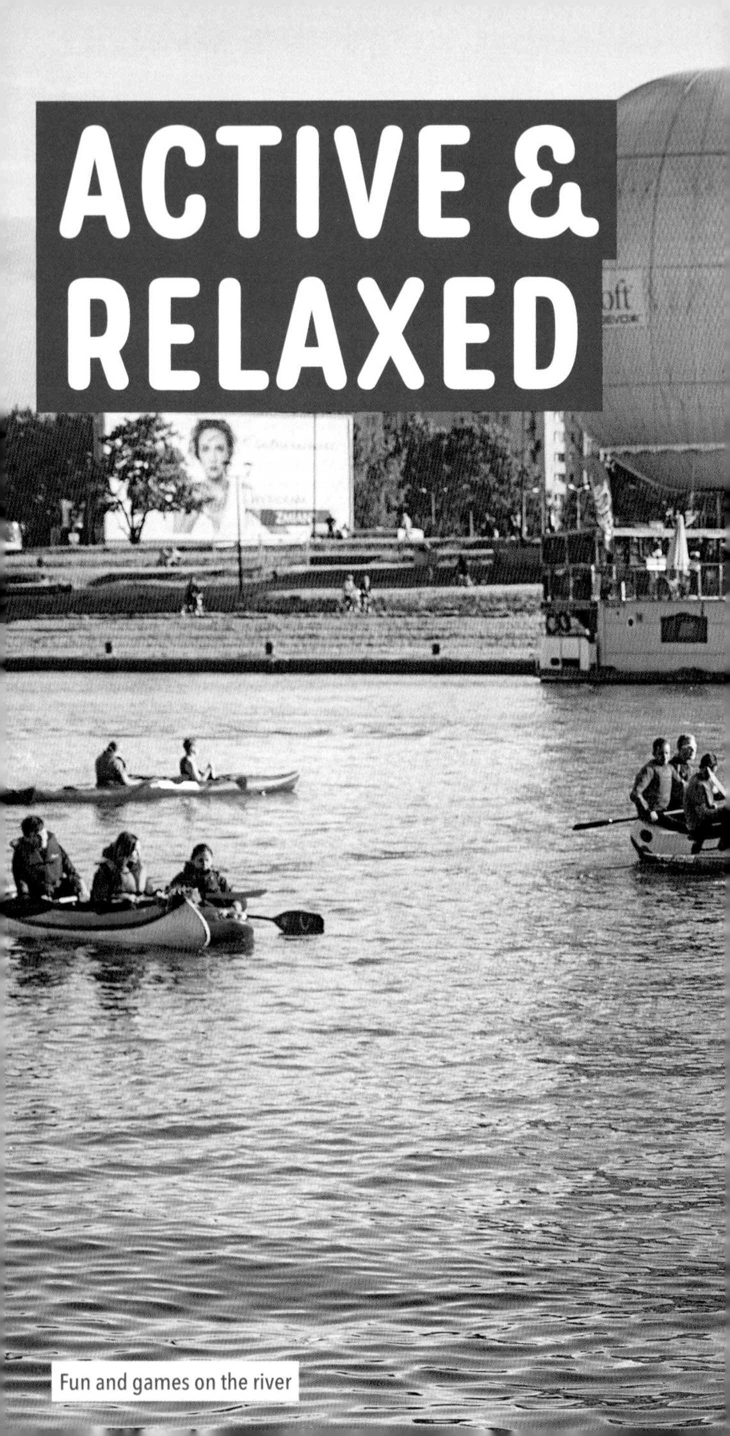

Fun and games on the river

BANKIETY / KONFERENCJE / NOCLEGI

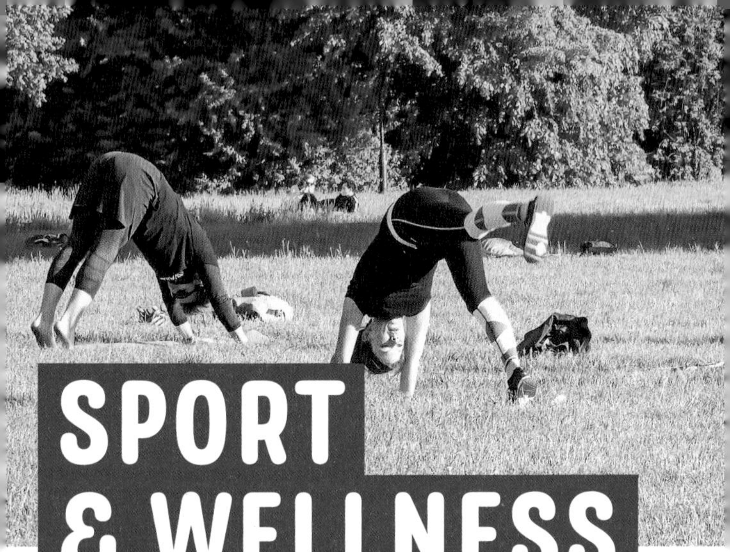

SPORT & WELLNESS

CANOEING

For a change from pounding the city streets, why not try a canoe trip along the Vistula? There are two main benefits: first, you get to see Kraków from a whole new angle; and secondly, you get to properly unwind out on the water on a sunny day. *May–mid Sept Mon–Fri 10am–sundown, Sat/Sun from 9am | from 15 zł /hr | Ulica Księcia Józefa 24a | kajaki-krakow.pl | bus A 14, A 44 Kraków Malczewskiego | 🕮 c10*

INSIDER TIP
Kraków from the river

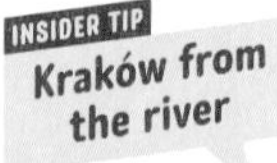

JOGGING & CYCLING

If you're craving a good workout, the best jogging and cycling routes are around *Błonia (🕮 c9)*. The tracks on the edge of the Old Town run along the Rudawa river at times and pass through 48 hectares of meadows, which are also the perfect place for the kids to let off steam.

The city's most beautiful *cycling tour* takes you along the Vistula river from Kraków towards the Benedictine Abbey of Tyniec. And don't worry if you can't be bothered to cycle back – just jump on one of the ferries docked along the river.

INSIDER TIP
Cycle by the river

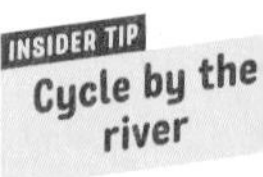

PARK JORDANA

This 20-hectare park has footpaths, children's playgrounds, football and volleyball pitches, as well as a small lake where kids can have fun in pedalos. Opened in 1889, it's Poland's oldest park and was created as a place for children and young people to play and do sport. *Ulica Ingardena | tram 15, 18 Park Jordana | 🕮 c9*

WATER PARK

Poland's largest indoor water park, *Aquapark* has swimming pools that

Park Jordana is perfect for open-air yoga

cover over more than 2,000m². The main attraction is the 200m-long water slide. There's also plenty here for parents, including yoga and tai-chi sessions. Adults can also choose to tone up in the fitness rooms or relax in the sauna. If hungry, you'll find a restaurant, café and several small shops on site. *Daily 8am–10pm | admission from 51 zł per hr, 8–9am 38 zł, family ticket (3 people) 129 zł/hr, additional offers on website | Ulica Dobrego Pasterza 126 | parkwodny.pl | 🕮 0*

WELLNESS

Farmona Wellness & Spa (Tue–Sun 9am–9pm | Ulica Jugowicka 10c | tel. 1 22 52 70 20 | spakrakow.pl | bus 244 Jugowicka | 🕮 c11), in the hotel of the same name, is a genuine feel-good oasis. You will be pampered all day long with special treatments from Bali and Hawaii, such as massages with hot stones and fragrant oils followed by aromatic baths.

YOGA & FITNESS

Jogacentrum (daily 8am–2pm, 5–10pm | Ulica Biskupia 18 | jogacentrum.org | 🕮 C4) is Kraków's oldest yoga school. It may have just two rooms, but they are beautiful and well kept, and the dedicated teachers create a great atmosphere. Meditation, Tibetan concerts, massages and lessons in English round off the programme.

At *Fitness Młyn (Ulica Dolnych Młynów 5 | fitnessmlyn.pl | 🕮 A–B5)*, we recommend booking a private pilates or yoga class (from 190 *zł*). All the trainers at this stunning studio speak English. Plus, if you are on the hunt for a jogging or workout buddy, the studio is also a good place to start.

FESTIVALS & EVENTS

MARCH/APRIL

Dni Bachowskie (Bach Days) are organised by the Kraków Music Academy. There are performances of Baroque music (not only by Bach) by Kraków students and other musicians, plus lectures. *amuz.krakow.pl*

Misteria Paschalia is a week-long festival with classical concerts in churches, the Kraków Philharmonic and the opera house. Theme: Lent and Easter. *misteriapaschalia.pl*

Starzy i Mlodzi czyli Jazz w Krakowie (Old and New – Jazz in Kraków) sees famous and not-so-famous musicians give concerts in jazz cellars, clubs and cafés at this international festival. *krakow-jazz.pl*

MAY

You can visit most of the city's museums (almost) free of charge on the **Noc Muzeów w Krakowie (Long Night of the Museums)**. A specially minted 1 *zł* coin is your admission ticket. This event is extremely popular, so you should expect long queues at the various museums.

JUNE

Concerts, parades, marathons and various other events are all part of the **Święto Miasta (City Festival)** at the beginning of June. The highlight is the **Parada Smoków (Dragon Parade)**, in which participants pull gigantic, colourful dragons through Kraków's streets.

The **Wianki (Vistula Wreath Festival)** at midsummer harks back to pagan days, when young girls cast wreaths into the water on the longest night of the year in the hope that fate would send them a loving husband. Also on the programme are concerts by familiar and unknown Polish bands and a firework display. *kbf.krakow.pl/en*

The sights and sounds of the Dragon Parade

Kazimierz celebrates the annual ★ **Festiwal Kultury Żydowskiej (Festival of Jewish Culture)** with concerts, films and exhibitions. There are also fascinating guided tours to places that are otherwise closed. *jewishfestival.pl*

AUGUST

Targi Sztuki Ludowej (Folk Art Markets) focus on the arts and crafts of Kraków. Traditional products made of wood and clay are sold on Rynek Główny.

SEPTEMBER

On the first Sunday of the month, you'll witness thousands of dog owners showing off their costumed darlings at the **Marsz Jamników (Dachshund Parade).**

The **Festival Sacrum Profanum** is a week-long music festival held in unusual locations, such as the former Schindler Factory and the steelworks in Nowa Huta. You'll hear all genres of music, ranging from jazz to electronic. There's also classical music, ballet and jazz at the Philharmonic Hall. *sacrumprofanum.pl*

INSIDER TIP
Music in unexpected locations

DECEMBER

On the first Thursday in December, makers display nativity cribs on Market Square. The best are picked at the *Konkurs Szopek Krakowskich (Christmas Nativity Contest)* and then exhibited in the **Krzysztofory Palace**, part of the **Museum of Kraków** *(Rynek Główny 35 | muzeumkrakowa.pl/en)*

INSIDER TIP
Top cribs in town!

From the second Saturday of the month the **Christmas Market** takes over Market Square

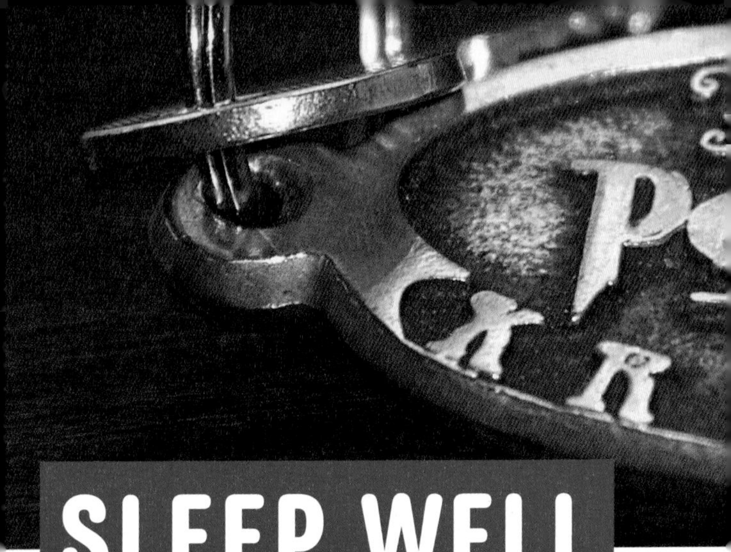

SLEEP WELL

HISTORY IN STYLE

Pod Różą (57 rooms | Ulica Floriańska 14 | tel. 1 24 24 33 00 | hotel.com.pl | 📖 d3) is the oldest hotel in Kraków: even Honoré de Balzac has laid his head here. The original architecture of the 15th-century townhouse on the Royal Route was combined with the luxury and comfort of the 21st century to create this hotel. There's a fine restaurant with a large wine cellar.

MAKE YOURSELF AT HOME

The apartments and studios in *Apartamenty Bracka 6 (16 apartments | Ulica Bracka 6 | tel. 1 23 41 40 11 | bracka6.pl | 📖 c5)*, a 500-year-old townhouse in a prime location, have been renovated with painstaking care. They all have parquet floors and air-conditioning and some have a balcony. The rooms are equipped with a small kitchenette.

HISTORIC SPLENDOUR

This magnificent house built in 1834 has now been turned into the *Pollera (40 rooms | Ulica Szpitalna 30 | tel. 1 24 22 10 44 | pollera.pl | 📖 e2–3)*, a hotel in which you can feel the special atmosphere of times gone by. The stained-glass windows in the staircase, created by Stanisław Wyspiański, are beautiful examples of art nouveau. Thick red and green carpets, comfortable sofas and Tiffany-style lamps complete the flair of this historic building. The suites are exceptionally beautiful.

INSIDER TIP
Art nouveau stained glass

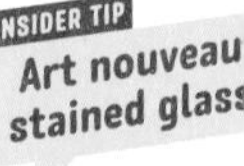

A NIGHT IN THE MUSEUM

Hotel Gródek (23 rooms | Ulica Na Gródku 4 | tel. 1 24 31 90 30 | donimirski.com | 📖 e4) is set in a Gothic building in a peaceful location in the heart of town. Each room has a

Old fashioned but stylish: Hotel Pollera

different interior design, and a Gothic church floor saved during renovations was laid in the reception area. The library has a wide selection of books and there's a lovely view of the Old Town from the charming restaurant. Objects found during renovations are on display, making this Poland's only private archaeological museum.

SLEEP LIKE A PRINCE

The property that houses the *Polski Pod Białym Orłem (54 rooms | Ulica Pijarska 17 | tel. 1 24 22 11 44 | donimirski.com | 🕮 d2)* has been in the possession of the Czartoryskis – a Polish aristocratic family – since 1913. It has a perfect location opposite St Florian's Gate in the middle of the Old Town, yet in the quiet pedestrian precinct. The suites, with their antique-style furnishings, are especially beautiful and the whole hotel is of a very high standard.

INSIDE EUROPE'S MOST BEAUTIFUL HOTEL

Once upon a time, there was a 16th-century townhouse that was chosen to become the most beautiful hotel in all of Europe. Granted, this happened quite some time ago, but staying at the *Stary Hotel (78 rooms | double rooms from 800 Pln | Ulica Szczepańska 5 | tel. 1 23 84 08 08 | stary.hotel.com.pl | 🕮 c3)* is still something like a dream – a journey back in time but with all modern amenities! Excellent comfort: dark wooden furniture, silk curtains, rare wooden parquet flooring and colourful marble bathrooms. The icing on the cake is the city view from the rooftop café's terrace – just heavenly!

INSIDER TIP
A room with a view

DISCOVERY TOURS

Want to get under the skin of the city? Then our discovery tours are the ideal guide – they provide advice on which sights to visit, tips on where to stop for that perfect holiday snap, a choice of the best places to eat and drink, and suggestions for fun activities

A duck's eye view of Wawel Hill

DISCOVERY TOURS OVERVIEW
Górka Narodowa
E77
7
79
W. E. Radzikowskiego
J. Conrada
Opolska
Azory
Krowodrza
Opolska
Bronowice Małe
Żabiniec
Balicka
Bronowicka
Łobzów
Olsza
Bronowice
Królewska
al. Armii Krajowej
Kleparz
Nawojki
Nowa Wieś
Czarnowiejska
Rudawa
Piastowska
Czarna Wieś
In the kings' garden
Połwsie Zwierzynieckie
Wesoła
al. marsz. F. Focha
al. Krasińskiego
Stare Miasto
T. Kościuszki
Zwierzyniec
J. Dietla
Dębniki
Kazimierz
księcia Józefa
780
B. Zielińskiego
Kraków at a glance
Tyniecka
Kalwar.
Kapelanka
Ludwinów
Wisła
History and modern art
Zakrzówek
Wyłom
Tyniecka
Norymberska
Kobierzyńska
Pychowice
S. Grota-Roweckiego
J. Brożka
Wadowicka
Łagiewniki
siostry
Kobierzyn
Zakopiańska
Wilga
W. Witosa
1 km
0.62 mi
Kurdwanów

Sudół
Zesławice
Powstańców
G. Morcinka
Mistrzejowice
Mistrzejowicka
Grębałów
Prądnik Czerwony
Bieńczyce
776
79
Kocmyrzowska
Dłubnia
Olsza II
Nowa Huta
Rakowice
Bieńczycka
2
al. Jana Pawła II
Nowohucka
aleja Pokoju
Contrasting districts: Kleparz and Nowa Huta
Dąbie
rzegórzki
Mogiła
Łęg
776
Ofiar Dąbia
Stoczniowców
Nowohucka
Powst. Wielkopolskich
al.
Wisła
Staw Płaszowski
Saska
Lipska
J. Surzyckiego
Płaszów
Zalew Bagry
Wielicka
Bieżanowska
Wola Duchacka
Prokocim
Nowosądecka
Wielicka
Piaski Wielkie

❶ KRAKÓW AT A GLANCE

➤ Journey through the centuries in the Old Town
➤ A true masterpiece: marvel at the Veit Stoss altarpiece
➤ Explore Jewish heritage in Kazimierz

Rynek Główny (Market Square)

Plac Nowy (New Square)

10km

1 day, walking time 2½ hours

❶ Rynek Główny

❷ Planty

❸ Wawel Hill

❹ St Mary's Church

❺ Café Szał

ROYAL VIEWS FROM WAWEL HILL

Start the day with breakfast on the main square ❶ Rynek Główny ➤ p. 32 at Kawiarnia Noworolski ➤ p. 63, a place harking back to Kraków's imperial and royal past. *Stroll along Ulica Sienna, and turn right through the landscaped park, the* ❷ Planty ➤ p. 37, *walking for 15 minutes until you reach the Wawel. You're now standing in front of* ❸ Wawel Hill ➤ p. 46, the former seat of the Polish kings. Visit Wawel Cathedral ➤ p. 42 and the Royal Castle ➤ p. 45. You'll have a magnificent view over the city and Vistula river from the Sigismund Tower. *Leave the hill via the* Dragon's Cave ➤ p. 46 *and see the* Wawel Dragon Statue as you emerge beside the river.

THE SPLENDOUR OF THE MIDDLE AGES

It's a 45-minute walk back to Rynek Główny, where you will discover a real masterpiece! Make your way into ❹ St Mary's Church ➤ p. 33 to see the world-famous Veit Stoss altarpiece. After exploring the splendid Gothic basilica, head up one of its towers and take in the beautiful view of the city. Every hour, the trumpet call from St Mary's, the hejnał ➤ p. 22, can be heard from the highest tower. The noon call is even broadcast nationwide on the radio. Listen in while stopping for a snack break on the roof terrace at ❺ Café Szał ➤ p. 35, *located in the Cloth Hall, just a short walk away.*

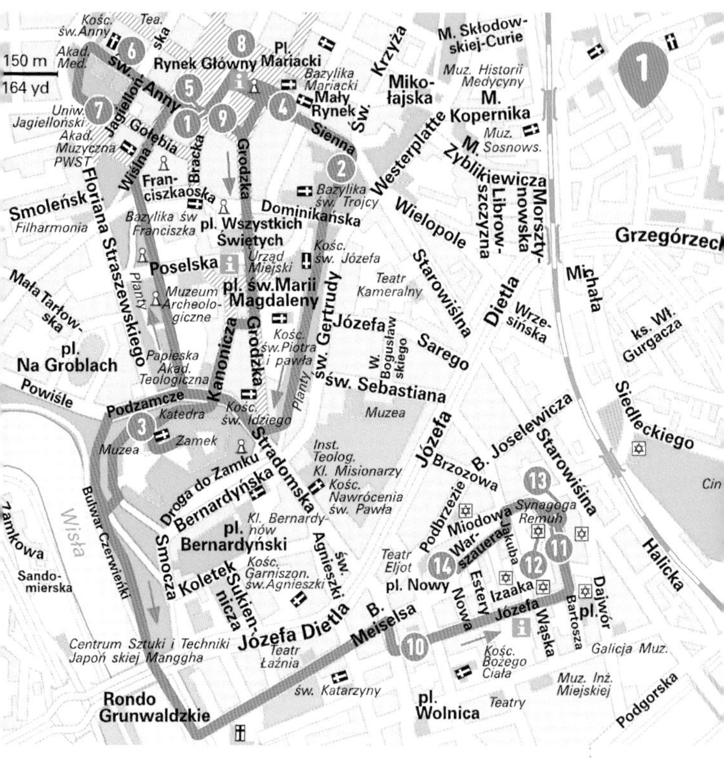

STUDIES OF OLD

Once fully refreshed, turn *into Ulica św. Anny at the southwest corner of Rynek Główny behind the Town Hall tower. Follow the street until you come to the magnificent Baroque* ❻ St Anne's Church ➤ p. 37, to your right. *To the left is the university building.* A visit to the museum in the ❼ Collegium Maius ➤ p. 36 will whisk you back to the Middle Ages. Don't miss the carillon in the university's inner courtyard, which chimes every two hours.

❻ St Anne's Church

❼ Collegium Maius

A CARRIAGE RIDE THROUGH THE CITY

From the heights of academia, *the tour now leads you under ground: the exhibition called* ❽ Rynek Underground ➤ p. 35 *in the* Cloth Hall ➤ p. 34, takes you through the city's hidden medieval streets. *Back at ground level* once more, the next stage of your journey

❽ Rynek Underground

⑨ carriage ride

back in time is about to begin. *Starting on Rynek Główny, embark on a* ⑨ carriage ride ➤ p. 117 back to the fin-de-siècle era at the end of the 19th century. *You travel along Ulica Grodzka and past the* Franciscan Church ➤ p. 36 *and the* St Peter & St Paul's Church ➤ p. 41. *After 30 minutes you reach the oldest street in the city,* Ulica Kanonicza ➤ p. 42, with its splendid episcopal palaces. *On foot, you now pass Wawel Hill to your right and keep going until you reach the riverbank and Bulwar Czerwieński, which you follow to the left. Keep walking along the Vistula until you turn left onto Ulica Paulińska after the Most Grunwaldzki bridge.*

IN THE FOOTSTEPS OF KRAKÓW'S JEWS

⑩ Ulica Józefa

⑪ Old Jewish Cemetery

⑫ Remuh Synagogue

⑬ Klezmer Hois

⑭ Plac Nowy

You're now walking into the heart of the former Jewish town of Kazimierz ➤ p. 46. *At the end of Paulińska, turn right onto Ulica Krakowska, then immediately left onto* ⑩ Ulica Józefa ➤ p. 72, *which leads to the* Synagoga Stara ➤ p. 49. The long street is lined with small but interesting shops, such as Szalom gallery, and vintage and jewellery stores like Blazko Jewellery ➤ p. 76. Before you leave this street, with its unique, hand-crafted souvenirs, have a look at the inner courtyard of the house at *Ulica Jóżefa 12*, where scenes from *Schindler's List* were filmed. *Walk past the Synagoga Stara and stop at the* ⑪ Old Jewish Cemetery ➤ p. 48. *Adjacent to the cemetery is the* ⑫ Remuh Synagogue ➤ p. 48. It's worth taking a look round the inside and visiting the shop for souvenirs, plus Jewish music and literature.

INSIDER TIP
Hollywood in Kraków

Take a carriage ride through town

KLEZMER AND CULT PUBS

The ⑬ Klezmer-Hois ➤ p. 68 is close by. Enjoy some Jewish specialities and, if you're lucky, listen to a klezmer concert. This is one of the city's trendiest districts, so enjoy the nightlife *around the bustling* ⑭ Plac Nowy ➤ p. 47 and head to the bar Alchemia ➤ p. 85 – a cult favourite!

2 CONTRASTING DISTRICTS: KLEPARZ AND NOWA HUTA

- Everyday hustle and bustle between the market and art school
- Picnic with rustic delicacies
- Explore the communist dream

Jama Michalika — Szara

21km — 1 day, walking time 2½ hours

FROM ART NOUVEAU TO THE ART OF TODAY

Start the day *at the* 1 Jama Michalika ➤ p. 62 café, one of the most famous art nouveau eateries in the city. *Following Ulica Florianska takes you to the remains of the* 2 city fortifications ➤ p. 38. *On the left-hand side,* artists have hung their paintings on the walls, creating a small open-air gallery. These works are for sale. *Before passing through* St Florian's Gate *and entering Kleparz, climb up the* Barbakane ➤ p. 38 for great views of the Kraków skyline.

1 Jama Michalika

2 city fortifications

STOCK UP FROM THE COUNTRY!

For many years, Kleparz was allowed to deteriorate, but now things have taken a turn for the better. *From the Barbican, cross Basztawa into* 3 Plac Jana Matejki (Matejko Square) with the huge Tannenberg Memorial and the fine neo-Renaissance home of the Kraków Art Academy *(Plac Matejki 13),* which was built in 1880. St Florian's Church *at the other end of the square* is also worth a visit – this is where the career of Karol Wojtyła, later Pope John Paul II, began. *Go back to Matejko Square and turn into Ulica Paderewskiego.* The largest 4 food market *(summer daily 9am–6pm, winter until 4pm | Plac Kleparski)* in the heart of the city now lies before you. Here you can purchase produce from farmers who may have travelled up to 100km: fruit and vegetables, of course, plus cheese from

3 Plac Jana Matejki

4 food market

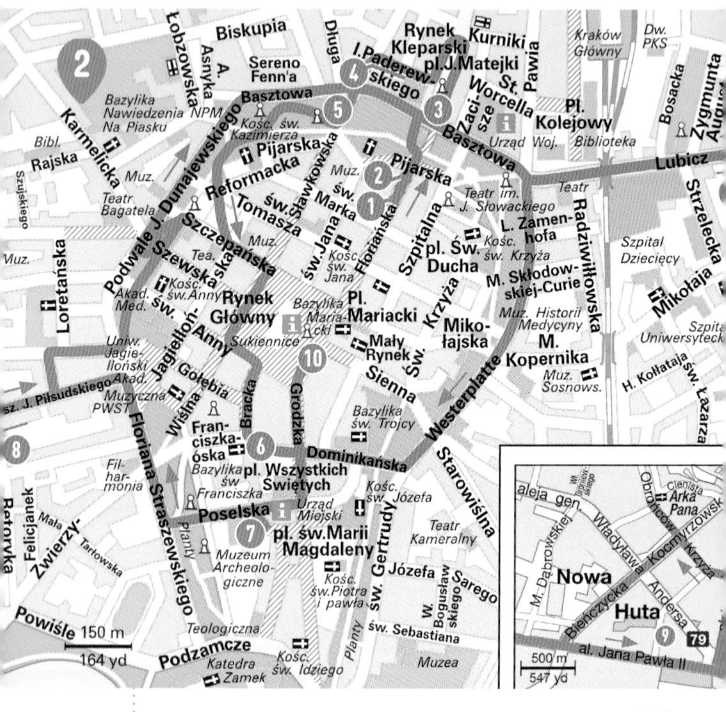

Zakopane, ham and bread. Stock up on provisions to take with you: home-made hummus, organic fruit juices, jams, sandwiches and coffee.

INSIDER TIP
Delicious food from the market

PICNIC BETWEEN THE SCULPTURES

5 Planty

The landscaped park, the 5 **Planty** ➤ p. 37 is directly in front of you and encircles the city. It is home to an interesting open-air exhibition of 19th- and 20th-century sculpture. *Stroll through the park* and stop for a picnic with your market purchases. After your meal, *carry on past the Baroque Church of St Casimir the Prince until you reach the* 6 **Franciscan Monastery**. Pop in to see the delightful stained-glass windows made by Stanislaw Wyspiański, an outstanding artistic talent who decisively influenced Kraków during the fin-de-siècle era.

6 Franciscan Monastery

AND NOW: MUSEUM TIME!

Get ready to enter another world on *Ulica Senacka*, the ⑦ Archaeological Museum *(Sept–June Tue, Thu 9am–5pm, Wed, Fri 9am–4pm, Sat/Sun 11am–4pm, July/Aug Tue–Fri 10am–5pm, Sat/Sun 10am–3pm | admission from 15 zł, Tue free | Ulica Senacka 3 | ma.krakow.pl)*. While here, not only will you learn about the region's prehistory and early history, but you'll find treasures from Ancient Egypt, too.

⑦ Archaeological Museum

Now *walk through Planty park again and along Ulica Straszewskiego. On Józefa Piłsudskiego, enter the main building of the* National Museum ➤ p. 52, *with its impressive collection of Polish artworks and crafts*. The ⑧ Art Book Store, the museum shop, is well worth a browse at the end of your visit. Afterwards, *continue along Szczepański Square, past the art nouveau Palace of Fine Arts and the Bunker of Arts*, which has made a name for itself with provocative contemporary exhibitions. *Back into the Planty, turn left and head for the tram stop Teatr Bagatela for the ride to Nowa Huta.*

⑧ Art Book Store

A PROLETARIAT PARADISE

A totally different Kraków lies in store for you in ⑨ Nowa Huta ➤ p. 54, the communist-built workers' town. *Get off the tram at the* Plac Centralny *and walk down* Aleja Róż ➤ p. 55 through the attractive, generously proportioned part of Nowa Huta, with its neoclassical-style houses from the 1950s and 1960s. *Turn left down Ulica Stefana Żeromskiego and continue straight ahead as far as the* Ark of the Lord Church ➤ p. 54. Inside, it's worth taking some time to explore and appreciate the modern interior of this church and its particularly impressive bronze sculpture of Christ.

⑨ Nowa Huta

⑩ Szara

Market provisions on Plac Kleparski

LUXURY ON A PLATE

Take the tram back to the city centre. The ⑩ Szara Gęś ➤ p. 67 restaurant, located in a medieval townhouse, provides the perfect contrast to Nowa

Huta. And seeing as you've done so much walking today, you deserve to treat yourself to a nightcap in the adjoining bar.

❸ IN THE KINGS' GARDEN

- Discover the vast Wolski Forest by bike
- Meet Kraków's animal residents at the zoo
- Pass beautiful villas in a charming residential area

Le Scandale — Plec Art

35km — 1 day, cycling time 2½ hours

Book in advance for the ❾ **Farmona Wellness & Spa.**

❶ Le Scandale
❷ Krk Bike Rental
❸ Biedronka
❹ Zwierzyniec

EXPLORE FORMER ROYAL HUNTING GROUNDS

Start with a hearty breakfast *at* ❶ Le Scandale ➤ p. 86. Next, rent an e-bike at ❷ Krk Bike Rental ➤ p. 114 as the tour will be hilly. Before you get started, make a *detour to the* ❸ Biedronka *(Rynek Główny 34)* supermarket to stock up on refreshments for the day. *Then ride through the Old Town and via Ulica Grodzka, past the Wawel and continue along the Vistula.* The district of ❹ Zwierzyniec (Zoo) includes the former hunting grounds and gardens of the Polish kings and the estates of the Klasztor Norbertanek (Convent of the Premonstratensian Nuns) and the Church of St Augustine & John the Baptist *(Ulica Kościuszki 88), which you reach after about ten minutes* (not open to the public).

VILLAS, AVENUES AND A BEAUTIFUL CEMETERY

Turn off to the right and cross over the road. On your left you'll see a rare example of sacred wooden architecture: *St Margaret's Church,* originally built in

the 17th century. Gracious buildings from the 19th and early 20th centuries, nestling in spacious parkland, dominate this residential suburb of Kraków. *Turn left into the pretty Ulica Gontyny. The route now takes you uphill into the Aleja Waszyngtona.* Soon, on the right-hand side, one of the oldest churches in the city comes into view, the Church of the Redeemer *(Ulica św. Bronisławy 9). As you continue along the chestnut-lined avenue, you pass the* ❺ Salwator Cemetery. Wander between the 19th-century graves; they include the last resting place of a number of Polish artists. *Carry on as far as the 34m-high* ❻ Kościuszko's Mound ➤ p. 22, which boasts a unique view of the city. Stop for lunch at the Restauracja pod Kopcem with the Panorama Café *(Mon–Fri from 11am, Sat/Sun from 10am | Aleja Waszyngtona | tel. 1 26 62 20 29 | restauracjapod kopcem.pl | ££)* in the renovated section of the fortified complex. The view is something else.

❺ Salwator Cemetery

❻ Kościuszko's Mound

MEET THE FOREST ... HIPPOS

Aleja Waszyngtona takes you deeper into the Las Wolski (Wolski Forest). At 425 hectares, it's the largest forest park in Poland. *A quarter of an hour later you*

7 Zoological Gardens

8 Decius Villa

9 Farmona Wellness & Spa

10 Piec Art

reach the 7 Zoological Gardens ➤ p. 56 – get ready to meet the colonies of hippopotamus, mouflon and tapir. *Afterwards, a further 15 minutes' cycling takes you to the* 8 Decius Villa, set in a delightful landscaped garden. *Following Ulica Królowej Jadwigi, Mydlnicka and the Aleja 3 Maja, your route takes you past the National Museum ➤ p. 52 and back to Ulica sw. Anny,* where you can return your bicycle.

WELLNESS, JAZZ AND GOOD FOOD

By now, you have well and truly earned a bit of pampering: take a taxi to 9 Farmona Wellness & Spa ➤ p. 91 and relax with a soothing massage. The day ends with an evening at 10 Piec Art ➤ p. 85, with a delicious meal, good cocktails and, if you're lucky, a jazz concert.

Kraków Zoo

4 HISTORY AND MODERN ART

- Thrilling finds on the Vistula's "other" bank
- Wander from Kazimierz to Podgórze
- Never again: the Nazi atrocities of the Kraków ghetto

Plac Wolnica | Gruzińskie Chaczapuri

6km | 1 day, walking time 1½ hours

ALL THINGS POLISH

Start your tour on the right bank of the Vistula at 1 Plac Wolnica in Kazimierz. Take time for breakfast at Urban Coffee *(daily from 8am | Plac Wolnica 12A | urbancoffee.pl)* and, suitably fortified, *walk towards the left-hand side of the square.* This is the site of the former Kazimierz Town Hall, which now houses the interesting 2 Ethnographic Museum *(Tue–Sun 10am–6pm | admission 18 zł | Plac Wolnica 7).* Admire the two floors of Polish folk art, traditional costumes and furniture. *After that, follow Ulica Bocheńska and turn into Ulica Mostowa* for a stopover at 3 Mostowa Art Café *(daily from noon | Ulica Mostowa 8 | FB: Mostowa Sztuka Kawa)* to try some local specialities.

1 Plac Wolnica

2 Ethnographic Museum

3 Mostowa Art Café

WANDER THE CITY, ICE-CREAM IN HAND

At the end of the street you can already make out the pedestrian bridge across the Vistula, the 4 Kładka Bernatka. *Once on the other side, walk down Ulica Brodzińskiego and Staromostowa,* where one of the unconventional ice-cream flavours at 5 Lody Si Gela ➤ p. 64 will sweeten the next stage of the walk. The largest church in the district, 6 St Joseph's Church *(Ulica Zamojskiego 2 | jozef.diecezja.pl),* stands on Rynek Podgórski. Directly behind the church, 7 Bednarski Park is the perfect place for a break after visiting the church and *before heading along Ulica Rękawka to Ulica Limanowskiego.* The area you are now in, Podgórze

4 Kładka Bernatka

5 Lody Si Gela

6 St Joseph's Church

7 Bednarski Park

⑧ Synagoga Zuckera

⑨ Cricoteka

⑩ Plac Bohaterów Getta

⑪ Eagle Pharmacy

⑫ Schindler Factory

➤ p. 54, was once the ghetto in which Kraków's Jewish population was interned from 1941 to 1943 under the Nazi regime. *Make a detour into Ulica Węgierska* to see the remains of the ⑧ Synagoga Zuckera, which was virtually destroyed by the Nazis. Today, the Galerie Starmach *(Mon–Fri 11am–5pm | Ulica Węgierska 5 | star-mach.com.pl)*, specialising in contemporary Polish art, is located behind the surviving façade.

DARK DAYS OF NAZI OCCUPATION

If you follow Ulica Limanowskiego, Węgierska and Józefinska, you'll come to the fabulous, ultra-modern art centre, the ⑨ Cricoteka ➤ p. 52, which will introduce you to the work of theatre director, painter and avant-garde artist Tadeusz Kantor, and give you a great view over the Vistula and Kazimierz. Having left the museum, *turn left and follow Ulica Nadwiślańska as far as Solna. On your right is* ⑩ Plac Bohaterów Getta (Ghetto Heroes Square) ➤ p. 54. The museum at the ⑪ Eagle Pharmacy ➤ p. 54 commemorates the area's devastating history. *Beyond the railway lines* are the buildings of the former ⑫ Schindler Factory ➤ p. 53. Here, the Museum of the City of Kraków presents its remarkable, "Kraków under Nazi Occupation 1939–1945" exhibition. Photographs taken during the making of the film *Schindler's List* hang in the museum café. At the

The Ghetto memorial on Plac Bohaterów

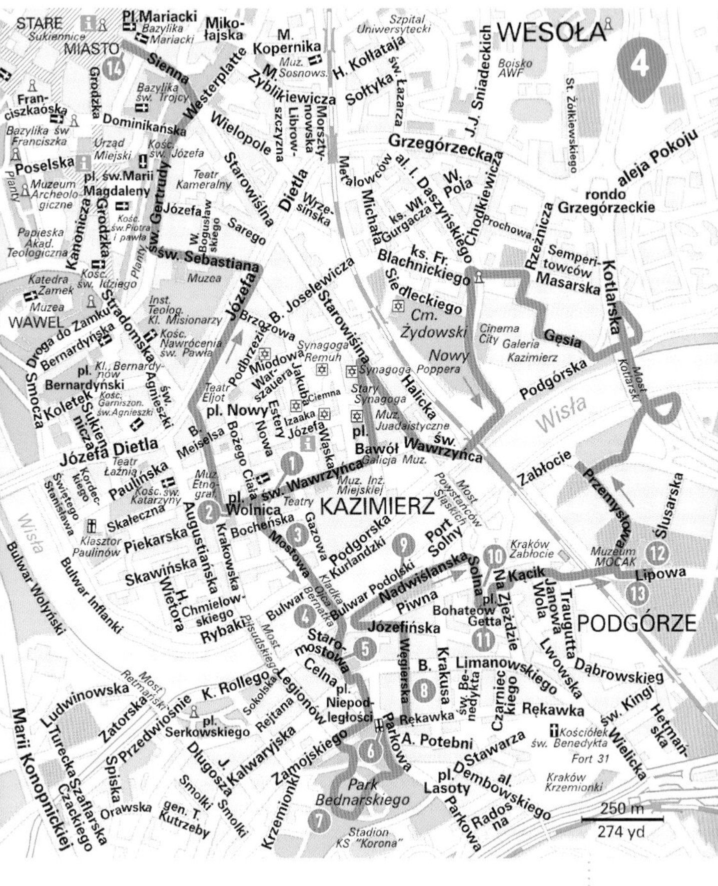

⑬ Glass Museum (*Mon–Fri 9am–5pm | admission 14 zł | Ulica Lipowa 3 | lipowa3.pl*) you can explore exhibitions on glass art, watch glass-blowers at work and have the chance to buy some unusual souvenirs.

SIDER TIP
ntricate and delicate souvenirs

⑬ Glass Museum

Take the Wow Kraków! Hop on Hop off Bus (from 100 zł /24 hours | tickets on the bus | wowkrakow.pl) from the Ulica Zabłocie 2 stop (a five-minute walk from the Glass Museum) back to the centre. Finally, bring your day to a close with some Georgian cooking at ⑭ Gruzińskie Chaczapuri (*daily from noon | Ulica Sienna 4 | tel. 1 24 29 11 66 | chaczapuri.pl*).

⑭ Gruzińskie Chaczapuri

GOOD TO KNOW

HOLIDAY BASICS

ARRIVAL

GETTING THERE

All national and international flights land at *Kraków Airport (krakowairport.pl)*. There are regular services from UK airports operated by the Polish national airline LOT *(lot.com)* and British Airways *(britishairways.com)*, as well as budget airlines EasyJet *(easyjet.com)* and Ryanair *(ryanair.com)*. It is sometimes possible to find very cheap fares, especially if you book ahead and out of season. LOT also offers direct flights from various US cities, and Ryanair offers direct flights from Dublin.

It is possible to reach Kraków from the UK by train. Take the Eurostar *(eurostar.com)* to Brussels, the high-speed train to Cologne, also run by Eurostar, and then the overnight sleeper train from Cologne to Warsaw. There are direct connections from Warsaw to Kraków. Alternatively, take the Eurostar to Paris and then the Nightjet sleeper train *(nachtzug.net/en)* from Paris to Berlin and an express train to Warsaw. For more train information, see *seat61.com*. International buses stop at the Kraków bus station *(Ulica Bosacka)*.

You can take bus 292 or 208 from the airport – both travel to the main train station in the centre of Kraków, Kraków Główny *(4 zł)*. You can also take the train directly from the airport to the station *(17 zł)*. The train departs every 30 minutes and the trip takes 16 minutes. A taxi to the centre of Kraków costs around 150 *zł*.

ENTRY REQUIREMENTS

EU citizens and Swiss nationals can use identity cards to enter Poland. Those from non-EU countries need passports to enter. In most cases, US and UK citizens can travel visa-free to Poland for stays of up to 90 days.

A summer view of the castle

GETTING AROUND

CAR

Driving in the city isn't recommended, but if you decide to do it, you will soon discover that parking in Kraków is anything but easy. The inner city is divided into three parking zones. Zone A (centre, red) is reserved for pedestrians; you are only allowed to drive to your hotel to unload your luggage, with parking strictly prohibited. There is a speed limit of 20kmh in Zone B (green) and you are only permitted to park at a very limited number of marked spaces. Parking is permitted in Zone C (blue, Mon–Sat 10am–8pm) after you have paid the appropriate fee. You can buy parking tickets from machines (they only take cash and change isn't given). If you are going to drive, it's a good idea to ask about parking facilities when you book your hotel.

If you're travelling outside the city, the speed limit on motorways is 140kmh in built-up areas (white signs) and 50kmh within towns (green signs), with a 60kmh limit from 11pm to 6am. There are frequent speed checks! Dipped beams are obligatory during the day and there must be a reflective vest in the boot.

PUBLIC TRANSPORT

You'll spend most of your time in Kraków on foot, as most sights in and around the Old Town are easily accessible. That's why we have only included public transport information where it's too far to walk from the city centre. If you want to visit the outskirts, then it's fastest and cheapest to travel by bus or tram; most run until around 11pm, when (infrequent) night buses

RESPONSIBLE TRAVEL

It doesn't take a lot to be environmentally friendly while travelling. Don't just think about your carbon footprint when flying to and from your holiday destination, but also about how you can protect nature and culture abroad. As a tourist it is especially important to respect nature, look out for local products, cycle instead of drive, save water and much more. To find out more about eco-tourism please visit: *ecotourism.org*.

begin to operate (their numbers start with 6). The cheapest ticket *(billet autobusowy)*, usable on both buses and trams, costs 4 *zł* and is valid for 20 minutes. You can buy tickets from machines and some *trafik* – kiosks that sell newspapers, cigarettes and drinks. There are also two ticket booths in the city centre: *Ulica Podwale 3/5* and *Ulica Mogilska 15a (both Mon–Fri 7am–7pm)*. A 20-minute ticket is valid for one journey; you have to buy another one if you change. In such cases, it is better to buy a 60- or 90-minute ticket that includes changes *(6/8 zł)*. Also available are 24-, 48- and 72-hour tickets *(22 zł, 35 zł and 50 zł)*.

CYCLING

There are only around 30km of marked cycle lanes in Kraków, but at least the city is nice and flat! The prettiest and safest places to ride are along the Vistula (to Tyniec or Nowa Huta), in Błonia, the Planty and in Las Wolski (Wolski Forest). This area has a lot of steep inclines, so mountain bikes and e-bikes are recommended. The average price to rent a bike is 50 to 60 *zł* per day. E-bikes are around 100 *zł*/day.

The most central bike hire venue is *Krk Bike Rental (daily 9am–sundown | Ulica św. Anny 4 | bike-rental.pl, 📖 D5)*. Mountain bikes and e-bikes are also available. In Kazimierz, you'll find *Dwa koła (Mon–Fri 9am–5pm, Sat 10am–2pm | Ulica Józefa 5 | dwakola.internetdsl.pl | 📖 E8)*. We also recommend *Art-Bike (Mon–Fri 10am–6pm | Ulica Starowiślna 33a | 📖 F7)*.

TAXIS

Taxis are relatively inexpensive. There are several taxi ranks in the city centre, and elsewhere you can use your mobile phone to call one *(Mega Taxi tel. 19625 or Barbakar tel. 19661)*. Normally, the taxi's meter is turned on: it usually shows 9 *zł* when you get in, and then there is a per kilometre charge starting at 3 *zł* depending on the tariff (weekday or weekend, holiday, day/night rate). On Sundays or after 10pm the rate is around twice as much as the normal daytime rate.

ESSENTIALS

BANKS & CURRENCY EXCHANGE

There are branches of many major Polish and European banks in Kraków *(usually Mon–Fri 7.30am–5pm, Sat 7.30am–2pm)* as well as privately operated exchange offices, called *kantor (daily 9am–7pm)*. However, it is much less complicated to take money from one of the many cash dispensers in the city using your debit or credit card.

CUSTOMS

The allowance when returning to the UK from Poland is 4 litres of spirits, plus 42 litres of beer and 18 litres of wine, and 200 cigarettes. For more information see *hmrc.gov.uk/customs*.

Travellers from the United States who are returning residents of the country do not have to pay duty on articles purchased overseas up to the value of $800, but there are limits on the amount of alcoholic beverages and tobacco products. For the regulations for international travel for US residents please see *cbp.gov*.

It is necessary to get authorisation from the Polish Ministry of Culture if you wish to export any objects made before 9 May 1945.

INFORMATION

They're hard to tell apart, but there are many public *(informacja)* and private tourist information offices in the centre of Kraków. The private ones also offer tours, including excursions to Zakopane, Wieliczka, Auschwitz and other destinations. Centres also sell tickets for concerts and events. *Tourist Information MCIT (Małopolskie Centrum Informacji Turystycznej | Rynek Główny 1/3 | Cloth Hall)*. Visit *infokrakow.pl* for a list of all information centres.

The *Karnet Magazin*, a brochure listing events in the city in Polish and

There's no need for a car to explore Kraków's neighbourhoods

View the sights at a trot

English, is published monthly and is available at *Ulica Jana 2*.

INTERNET & WIFI

All the tourist information centres, many cafés and most restaurants provide free Internet access. A password, which you will be given free of charge by the waiter or waitress (for a limited period), is usually necessary. Internet cafés are now uncommon in Kraków.

LUGGAGE STORAGE

Book your storage online here: *short.travel/kra18*. There are dozens of options near the main sights or transport hubs. Cost per day is around 22 *zł*.

MONEY & CREDIT CARDS

Poland's national currency is the *złoty (zł)*. One *złoty* is made up of 100 *groszy*. It is sometimes possible to pay in euros (notes only) in Kraków, but change is given in *złoty*.

OPENING HOURS

While shops used to stay open all weekend, a new trading law has restricted Sunday trading hours. However, the restricted hours don't apply to every business (for example, bakeries and petrol stations are exempt) and there are several Sundays a year when all shops are allowed to open. Search online to discover these dates.

During the week, most shops open from 10am to 6pm and on Saturday, from 10am to 3pm. Some food shops in the town centre stay open until 10pm, with some even operating 24/7. Large shopping centres and chain

stores are open until 10pm during the week and 8pm on Saturday.

PHONE & MOBILES

Dialling code for Australia *0061*, Canada *001*, Ireland *00353*, UK *0044*, USA *001*. Dialling code for Poland *0048*.

Some UK phone companies offer free roaming in the EU; check before travelling. It may be cheaper to make calls using a Polish prepaid SIM (for example, a "karta SIM" from the post office). SIM cards must be registered in person, so buying one can take time.

POST

You can purchase stamps and envelopes from post offices *(poczta)*. The most central ones are *Plac Wszystkich Świętych 9 (Mon–Fri 11am–7pm)* and the *main post office (Mon–Fri 8am–8pm, Sat 8am–2pm | Wielopole 2)*. Near the main train station is a 24-hour post office *(Ulica Lubicz 4)*. Postcards and letters up to 50g cost 8 *zł* for any European destination.

PUBLIC HOLIDAYS

1 Jan	New Year's Day
March/April	Easter Monday
1 May	Labour Day
3 May	Constitution Day
May/June	Corpus Christi
15 Aug	Assumption
1 Nov	All Saints' Day
11 Nov	Independence Day
25/26 Dec	Christmas

SAFETY

Kraków is one of the safest towns in Poland, but here – as everywhere – it's still good to be aware of your surroundings. Watch out for pickpockets in large crowds, especially in busy pubs, clubs and bars. There are usually no problems in the inner city at night, but you should avoid districts such as Nowa Huta and Podgórze when it is dark, or take a taxi.

SIGHTSEEING & CITY TOURS

Electrically powered Melex vehicles, similar to large golf carts, drive around the city on fixed routes *(from 40 zł, krakowzwiedzanie.pl/en)*, taking in the main tourist sights.

How much the *Cracow Free Tours (freewalkingtour.com)* costs is entirely up to you – you pay by donation. There's a two-hour tour through the Old Town on Friday, Saturday and Sunday, for example, which starts every day at 10am at the Kraków Barbican, and an afternoon excursion to Kazimierz (2pm), both in English. Be prepared that you will be part of a large group.

You can take a hop-on/hop-off bus tour on a red open-top bus (with a retractable roof) with *WOWKrakow! (daily 9.30am-6pm | wowkrakow.pl)* Tickets are available online, on the bus or at several points of sale, and are valid for one or two days *(100 or 150 zł)*. You can get on and off as often as you'd like. A single tour *(60 zł)* is also available. See website for the route.

The *Communism Tour (2.5 hours | £140 for 1, £150 for 2, £170 for 3, with larger groups also catered for)* of Nowa Huta by *Crazy Guides (crazyguides.com)* invokes the history of the district between 1945 and 1989. This, their most popular tour, in a vintage Trabant or Polish Fiat 126p (known as the "Toddler"), includes lunch and a visit to an apartment furnished in the style of the time.

A ride in a *horse-drawn carriage (30 mins, from Market Square to the Wawel | 150 zł)* for 4–5 passengers, is a good way to see the city.

Officially, only licensed guides are allowed to give city tours of Kraków. Book through the *Marco der Pole travel agency (krakow-travel.com, marcoderpole.com.pl)*. Joanna Tumielewicz, the author of this guide, also shows visitors round the city *(tel. 5 05 03 31 31 | tumielewiczj@interia.pl)*.

From April to October, you can discover Kraków from the river, *(Bulwar Czerwieński 3 | dock Przystań Wawel, near Grunwaldzki Bridge | tel. 5 30 75 07 36 | statekkrakow.com)*. One-hour cruises start between 9am and 6pm and cost 90 zł. The four-hour trip *(May–Oct daily, see website for departure times | 160 zł)* is combined with an hour's stop at the Benedictine abbey in Tyniec.

Cracow City Tours (tel. 124 21 13 33 | cracowcitytours.com) offers tours to Auschwitz *(from 170 zł | start: Plac Matejki 2)*. The total travel time is around three hours, and you'll need another three hours to tour the site.

TICKETS

Almost all museums offer free entry to their permanent exhibitions on Tuesdays, and many are closed on Mondays. As is the case wherever you go, buying tickets online in advance will make life easier. Use the website *bilety.mnk.pl* for all parts of the National Museum.

HOW MUCH DOES IT COST?

Beer	*from £2/$3.10 for 0.5 litres in a restaurant*
Cappuccino	*from £1.60/$2.50 for a cup in a café*
Pizza	*from £5/$8 in a restaurant*
Club	*from £5/$6 per person*
Museum	*from £1/$1.60 per person*
Bus	*from £0.80/$1 for one trip*

TIPPING

Tips are not included on the bill in cafés and eateries, and it is customary to round it up. In higher-class restaurants, a 10% tip is usual, provided you are satisfied with the service.

EMERGENCIES

CONSULATES AND EMBASSIES

BRITISH EMBASSY

Ulica Kawalerii 12, 00-468 Warsaw | tel. +48 22 311 00 00 | ukinpoland.fco.gov.uk/en/

U.S. CONSULATE GENERAL

Ulica Stolarska 9, 31-043 Kraków | tel. +48 124 24 51 00 | poland.usembassy.gov

CANADIAN EMBASSY

Ulica Jana Matejki 1/5, 00-481 Warsaw | tel. +48 225 84 31 00 | canadainternational.gc.ca/poland-pologne

EMERGENCY NUMBERS

General emergency number: *112*. Tourist emergencies (daily 8am–6pm, June–Sept until 8pm): *tel. 2 22 78 77 77* (landline) or *6 08 59 99 99* (mobile).

HEALTHCARE

UK travellers can use a UK Global Health Insurance Card (GHIC) to obtain basic emergency healthcare. However, they should also obtain private travel insurance, with a medical component, before travelling. US residents should obtain private health insurance. EU residents can use a European Health Insurance Card (EHIC), which guarantees treatment for those legally insured; the costs are refunded in keeping with the rates in your home country. Travel insurance is necessary for any additional services.

WEATHER IN KRAKÓW

High season
Low season

	JAN	FEB	MARCH	APRIL	MAY	JUNE	JULY	AUG	SEPT	OCT	NOV	DEC
Daytime temperatures	-1°	2°	7°	14°	19°	22°	24°	24°	20°	13°	7°	2°
Night-time temperatures	-6°	-5°	-1°	4°	9°	12°	15°	14°	10°	5°	1°	-3°
Hours of sunshine per day	1	2	3	5	6	7	7	6	5	3	2	1
Rainy days per month	8	7	8	8	11	12	10	9	8	8	9	10

Hours of sunshine per day   Rainy days per month

WORDS & PHRASES IN POLISH

SMALL TALK

yes/no/maybe	tak/nie/może
please/thank you	proszę/dziękuję
Hello/Hi!	Witam!/Cześć!
Good morning/day/ evening/night!	Dzień dobry!/Dobry wieczór!/Dobranoc!
Goodbye!	Do widzenia!
I am called …	Nazywam się …
What's your name?	Jak się nazywasz?
I'm coming from…	Pochodzę z …
Excuse me!	Przepraszam!
I'm sorry, what?	Słucham?
I don't like that.	To mi się nie podoba.
I would like …	Chciałbym *(m)*/ Chciałabym *(f)*…

SYMBOLS

EATING & DRINKING

Could we please reserve a table for four people for this evening?	**Proszę zarezerwować dla nas na dziś wieczór stolik dla czterech osób.**
The menu, please.	**Czy mogę prosić kartę?**
Could I please have …?	**Chciałbym** *(m)* **…?/ Chciałabym** *(f)* **…?**
Vegetarian	**wegetarianin** *(m)***/ wegetarianka** *(f)*
I would like to pay, please.	**Proszę o rachunek.**
cash/credit card	**gotówka/karta kredytowa**

MISCELLANEOUS

Where is .../Where are ...?	**Gdzie jest ...?/ Gdzie są ...?**
What time is it?	**Która godzina?**
How much is ...?	**Ile kosztuje ...?**
Where can I get internet access?	**Gdzie znajdę dojście do internetu?**
timetable/ticket	**rozkład jazdy/bilet**
open/closed	**otwarte/zamknięte**
left/reight/straight ahead	**na lewo/na prawo/ prosto**
more/less	**więcej/mniej**
cheap/expensive	**tanio/drogo**
fever/pains	**gorączka/ból**
pharmacy/drugstore	**apteka/drogeria**
broken	**rozbity**
breakdown/garage	**awaria/warsztat**
Help!/Look out!	**Ratunku!/Uwaga!**
0/1/2/3/4/5/6/7/8/9/ 10/100/1000	**zero/jeden/dwa/ trzy/cztery/pięć/ sześć/siedem/osiem/ dziewięć/dziesięć/ sto/tysiąc**

HOLIDAY VIBES

FOR RELAXATION & CHILLING

FOR BOOKWORMS & FILM BUFFS

THE GIRL IN THE RED COAT
Roma Ligocka chillingly describes through the eyes of a child how she survived the horrors of the Holocaust in the Kraków Ghetto (2003).

THE ZONE OF INTEREST
Even Nazis read their children bedtime stories: Jonathan Glazer's double Oscar-winning film portrays the life of the family of Rudolf Höss, commandant of the Auschwitz concentration camp. His wife Hedwig's "paradise garden" borders directly on the camp – an idyll amid horror that is hard to bear (2023).

ANOTHER BEAUTY
Adam Zagajewski looks back on everyday life in Kraków in the 1960s, beautifully immortalising the people living in the city at the time – not least a priest named Karol Wojtyła (2000).

SCHINDLER'S LIST
Shot in Kraków, Steven Spielberg's film recounts the story of the 1,100 Jews saved by factory owner Oskar Schindler (1993).

PLAYLIST ON SHUFFLE

II KROKE & NIGEL KENNEDY – KAZIMIERZ
This Kraków Klezmer band joined forces with Nigel Kennedy, who has made the city his home, to take you on an aural journey into the area's Jewish past.

▶ MOTION TRIO – TRAIN TO HEAVEN
This Kraków trio showcases just how much you can do with an accordion.

▶ BOBA JAZZ BAND – SWEET SUE
Traditional jazz with plenty of swing.

▶ ZBIGNIEW WODECKI – CHAŁUPY WELCOME TO
This popular music icon was a gifted singer and multi-instrumentalist.

▶ MANAAM – KRAKOWSKI SPLEEN
Singer Kora, born Olga Jackowska in Kraków, lends her talent to this rock band to come up with a different sound.

The holiday soundtrack is available at **Spotify** under **MARCO POLO Poland**

Or scan the code with the Spotify app

ONLINE

KARNET.KRAKOW.PL/EN
Online magazine showcasing Kraków's varied cultural and entertainment scene, from music, literature, theatre and exhibitions to cinema and the various festivals. The website has a good search function.

KRAKOW.TRAVEL/EN
Attractive official city travel guide produced by the Kraków Festival Office.

KRAKOWPOST.COM
The latest city news on all kinds of subjects, with in-depth articles in English.

LOCAL-LIFE.COM/KRAKOW
A forum with a lively, well-informed and clearly organised English-language guide.

KRAKOW4U.PL
Dozens of fabulous photos of Kraków; the 360° shots of the sights are particularly impressive.

KRAKOWBUZZ.COM
Lots of rankings, including for hotels, restaurants and nightlife, plus great tips and information about Kraków's sights.

TRAVEL PURSUIT

THE MARCO POLO HOLIDAY QUIZ

Do you know what makes Kraków tick? Here you can test your knowledge of the little secrets and idiosyncrasies of this city and its people. The answers are at the bottom of the page, with further details on pages 18 to 23 of this guide.

❶ How did the brave cobbler bring down the evil dragon?
a) With a lance
b) With a sheep stuffed with sulphur, tar and pepper
c) He toppled him from Wawel Hill

❷ What was named after Pope John Paul II?
a) The city's botanical gardens
b) A church in Kraków's Old Town
c) A cream cake

❸ Who invaded Kraków in the 13th century?
a) Vandals
b) Mongols
c) Moors

❹ Which city was Kraków modelled on during the period of the Austro-Hungarian Empire?
a) Vienna
b) Budapest
c) Prague

❺ What's the Polish name for the river that flows through Kraków?
a) Odra
b) Motława
c) Wisła

❻ What's the *hejnał*?
a) A meat dumpling
b) A trumpet call
c) A famous artwork in the National Museum

Answers: 1 b, 2 c, 3b, 4 a, 5 c, 6 b, 7 b, 8 a, 9 b, 10 c, 11 b

Tales of dragons abound in Kraków

❼ **Which Kraków work of art was sculptor Veit Stoss responsible for?**

a) An amber effigy of Pope John Paul II

b) The main altar in St Mary's Church

c) A communist monument in Nowa Huta

❽ **What parades through the city in colourful fashion in summer?**

a) Dragons

b) Witches

c) Knights and kings

❾ **Who was the artist who shaped Kraków's cultural scene towards the end of the 19th century?**

a) Karol Wojtyła

b) Stanisław Wyspiański

c) Lech Wałęsa

❿ **What is the name for traditional Jewish music?**

a) Swing

b) Jazz

c) Klezmer

⓫ **Why aren't the pigeons chased away from Market Square?**

a) Because they are a protected species

b) Because legend has it that they are knights caught under a witch's spell

c) Because they are the city's heraldic animal

INDEX

WE WANT TO HEAR FROM YOU!

Did you have a great holiday? Is there something on your mind? Whatever it is, let us know! Whether you want to praise the guide, alert us to errors or give us a personal tip – MARCO POLO would be pleased to hear from you.
Please contact us by email:

sales@heartwoodpublishing.co.uk

We do everything we can to provide the very latest information for your trip. Nevertheless, despite all of our authors' thorough research, errors can creep in. MARCO POLO does not accept any liability for this.

PICTURE CREDITS
Cover photo: St Mary's Church (AWL Images/ ImageBROKER: C. Handl)
Photos: R. Freyer (13); huber-images: G. Filippini (14/15); Laif: P. Hirth (16/17, 53, 58/59, 78/79, 87, 96/97); Laif/hemis: P. Hauser (69); Laif/Robert Harding Productions/robertharding (70/71); Look: K. Maeritz (48, 63, 84), T. Stankiewicz (34); Look/age fotostock (23, 27); K. Maeritz (4, 33, 40, 44); mauritius imag-es/AA World Travel Library/Alamy (12, 55); mauritius images/age: M. Larys (47); mauritius images/ Alamy: © Bill Bachmann (116/117), G. Berg (75), I. G. Dagnall (28/29), M. Kanning (94/95), K. Labunskiy (105), Little valleys (37), Pegaz (67), J. Ritterbach (20/21, 57), W. Skrypczak (10), G. Tsichlis (122/123), ZUMA Press, Inc (92/93); mauritius images/Digital-Fotofusion Gallery/Alamy (38); mauritius images/ Hemis.fr: R. Mattes (6/7); mauritius images/les polders/Alamy (110); mauritius images/robertharding: C. Mouyiaris (8/9, 102); mauritius/John Warburton-Lee: K. Garrod (76); Shutterstock: Anpopiel (124/125), badahos (24), De Visu (88/89), hurricanehank (82/83), E. Krzysztof (90/91), M. Krzyzak (112/113), MarKord (64), Olivier Uchmanski (6/7), Sopotnicki (11), D. Turbasa (outside flap, inside flap); Shutterstock/ kronikarz.com (2/3); Shutterstock/travellifestyle (108, 115); Shutterstuck: D. Pietruszka (50); J. Tumielewicz (127)

4th Edition – fully revised and updated 2024
Worldwide Distribution: Heartwood Publishing Ltd, Bath, United Kingdom
www.heartwoodpublishing.co.uk

Author: Joanna Tumielewicz
Editor: Jens Bey
Picture editor: Susanne Mack
Cartography: © 2024 KOMPASS-Karten GmbH, A-6020 Innsbruck; MAIRDUMONT, D-73751 Ostfildern (pp. 98–99, 101, 104, 107, 111, inside cover, outside cover, pull-out map); © 2024 KOMPASS-Karten GmbH, kompass.de using map data from © OpenStreetMap Contributors, osm.org/copyright (pp. 30–31, 35, 43, 49, 60–61, 72–73, 80–81).
Cover design and pull-out map cover design: bilekjaeger_Kreativagentur with Zukunftswerkstatt, Stuttgart
Page design: Langenstein Communication GmbH, Ludwigsburg

Heartwood Publishing credits:
Translated from the German by Madeleine Oldham, Susan Jones
Editors: Rosamund Sales, Kate Michell, Felicity Laughton, Sophie Blacksell Jones
Prepress: Summerlane Books, Bath
Printed in India

MARCO POLO AUTHOR
JOANNA TUMIELEWICZ
Born and bred in Kraków, Joanna Tumielewicz is passionate about her city, guiding guests from abroad through its romantic alleyways and magnificent churches. The German specialist and art historian works as a city guide and translator, and enjoys art, cinema and literature. She lives with her family (and many pets!) in the Wola Jusowska district of Kraków.

DOS & DON'TS

HOW TO AVOID SLIP-UPS & BLUNDERS

DON'T MAKE JOKES ABOUT THE CHURCH

Around 98% of the Poles are Roman Catholic and the Church still plays a major role in society. So even if the locals make jokes about priests and the Church, you should resist any temptation to do the same.

DON'T GRIPE

Kraków residents know that things are still not perfect in their city. Poles like to grouse themselves, but don't take kindly to criticism from foreigners. Concentrate on the many positive things you experience instead.

DO DRESS MODESTLY TO ENTER A CHURCH

Being a tourist is no excuse for not observing the rule of not wearing shorts or sleeveless garments when you visit a church. You will either not be allowed to enter or asked to put something on. Some churches, such as St Mary's, will provide you with a shawl. And don't forget to take your hat off!

DON'T DRINK ALCOHOL IN PUBLIC OR LITTER THE STREETS

In Poland, it is forbidden to drink alcohol in public and to smoke at public transport stops. Kraków is a clean city and there are rubbish bins on every corner. You will be fined if you are caught throwing away a cigarette butt.

DON'T PARK ILLEGALLY

Kraków is divided into three parking zones, and you can only park in Zones 2 and 3 if you have a valid parking ticket. If you park your car illegally or without a ticket, a wheel clamp will make it impossible for you to drive away – and it will be very expensive to have it removed!